May 2020

To Camielle Jolly:
Congratulations on Your
Graduation. May the Lord
bless and guide your future
with His!!
Love, Uncle Mike Harp

Windows to Our World
Sarah's Journal

Growing Up, Crossing Oceans, Finding Love
& Giving Life to 10 Children
By Sarah Janisse Brown

Copyright 2014

Published by Thinking Tree Publishing, LLC
The Thinking Tree,LLC
617 N. Swope St.
Greenfield, IN 46140
United States
317.622.8852 PHONE (Dial +1 outside of the USA)
267.712.7889 FAX
www.ThinkingTreePress.com

ISBN-13:978-1502510112 • ISBN-10:1502510111

Cover photography by Joshua Pratt & Estera Brown
Editing by Charity Singleton Craig & Candace Nall
Graphic design by Clement Nicolle

WindowsToOurWorld.com

Sarah's Blog www.StillSMiling.net

All Scripture Quoted from the New King James Version Holy Bible

In compliance with the Fair Use Guidelines of Thomas Nelson Publishing

WINDOWS
—— TO OUR ——
W🌎RLD

SARAH JANISSE BROWN

sarah@stillsmiling.net

This book is dedicated
to my husband Joshua,
our children and generations
yet to come.

TABLE OF CONTENT

OPENING A WINDOW

My story did not begin on the day I was born, and it will not end with the last words of the last chapter in this book. Each chapter is a story. Each story is a window.

You are like a friend or stranger passing by my life, catching glimpses of my story on any given day. This book begins with me as a child, learning to paint with my mother, and follows me through decades and across oceans, now with my husband, Joshua, and our ten children. Joshua's mission in life is to make me smile, make God smile, and tell the world a story. I'll go anywhere with him.

But mine is a story that actually began many generations ago with the uncommon bravery of my grandmothers who came to America from many lands: Bohemia, Ireland, Poland, England, Italy, and other places unknown. I was told that my great, great grandmother left Italy about 100 years ago. I would love to pass by her house and look into her windows, but her story was never written. I can only imagine. Her journey across the ocean took months, not hours, like mine did. As I spent part of my days in her country, I wondered what her life was like and what she left behind. I realize that if it hadn't been for her courage to sail to America long ago I would not be writing this story today.

These ancestors of mine were immigrants, like I am now, strangers in a new land. They were the survivors who said many goodbyes. We said goodbye to all of our friends too, but we see their faces and keep up with them remotely every time we log into Facebook. They packed their trunks and boarded trains and ships for a better life. We came with our colorful backpacks and rolling suitcases. Some came with many children, like I did. Others barely escaped with the clothes on their backs, the babies in their arms, and the tears in their eyes. It was not for themselves that they crossed the great sea, but for their children and for their future generations, for me.

Their untold story brings me here. I am their story; they are mine.

I entered their—my—story in July 1976, and I began to cross the paths of their beginnings when I flew across the ocean as a teenager. Then, on an October night in 2012, above the clouds on an airplane, my husband and I and our family, became immigrants ourselves. We are travelers now, making our home wherever we go. For our children and their future generations.

We left the American Dream behind, living a new dream because we *are* Americans, free to live by faith, to show our children what exists on the other side of the world. I brought just a few things with me, mostly books—the journals I have filled with the stories from my own life. For me these are the windows to my past.

Now I have a pen in my hand, and I'm letting go of my story. I am tempted to hold onto my memories and keep secrets of my journey locked up in my heart, my love letters, and journals. But what good is a story unless it is told? So for you, for my children, and for their children, I am passing along a few pages of my life.

I hope you enjoy this part of my story as much as I have enjoyed the journey. Now let me open a window...

PART 1

GROWING UP

A BETTER PLACE

The world became a better place the day my mom brought baby Heather home from the hospital. Before then, I had been the baby to my three older sisters. Now I had my own baby sister. She was so beautiful, so tiny, and so cute. I remember how my mom would lay on the couch with baby Heather tucked in beside her with a big bowl of popcorn on the coffee table to share with me. Two of my favorite things in one place: babies and popcorn. Life couldn't have been better.

I always wanted to hold the baby. Sometimes I would climb up on the couch beside my mom, and my arms would ache with longing to rock that tiny baby. I loved the songs my mom would sing to her, and I wanted to sing those songs to the baby, too. Sometimes my mom or dad would read my mind and pass me the baby, and I would pretend like she was mine. I would look at her and think about how much I wanted to grow up and have lots of little babies to sing to. My mom had five daughters, and I was determined that when I grew up I would have at least six girls of my own.

At just three years old, I looked at the world very literally, filling in what was missing with my big imagination. I was a quiet observer, and I loved to watch people and listen in on the conversations around me. I began noticing that grown-ups said the strangest things. My grandmother once told my sister not to "let the cat out of the bag." That poor kitty! I was so worried! When I went looking for the cat, he wasn't in a bag after all. He was on the back of the couch. Maybe there was another cat, I thought, maybe it was going to be a birthday present. My dad warned my sisters not to get "hooked" on television, but I couldn't find any hooks on our console. My mom would talk about "fishing around" in the junk-drawer, but there were no fish there. I checked. My sisters would say things were "so cool," but when I would touch them, they weren't cold at all. I remember my dad talking about always being "broke," but he looked okay to me.

From a very young age my vivid imagination and gullibility led me to make some really strange conclusions about the world around me. Was my baby sister really as "cute as a button"? What did it mean to "fall in love"? Wasn't I too young to "drive my sister crazy"? I didn't have a cent but was often accused of "passing the buck." Did the lady at the store really want to "eat up" baby Heather? Trying to understand humans was no easy task. I would rather talk with the birds, lizards, and cats than try to understand people—unless they were babies of course!

In our home, we always gathered around the table at dinnertime. My dad loved to cook and would often bake chicken, make a big pot of chili, or throw together his famous rice and corn concoction that we kids called "stuff." My sisters would take turns mashing the potatoes. As soon as I was old enough, I helped make the biscuits and peel the carrots. I loved watching what happened to food when it was cooked. Things looked and tasted so different once they came out of the oven. My mom would always serve two different types of veggies and milk in every glass. I didn't like hot vegetables, so Mom let me eat mine raw. I loved to watch my parents in the kitchen together; they seemed to be having so much fun. All five of us girls learned to help, too. When we were old enough, Heather and I would set and clear the table; the big sisters— Sunny, Linda, and Charity—would clean the kitchen after the meal was done.

The two cats and dog would always come running when they would hear us sing our dinnertime songs. My Dad would sit at the head of the table, and we would all hold hands and pray. While we ate, we talked about our days. I did a lot more listening than talking. Sometimes, Dad would tell stories about the trouble he got into when he was a little boy. We would talk about summer vacation and ask for new pets. Anyone with bad manners was scolded by Dad, and no one would dare to talk with food in her mouth—only dads were allowed to do that.

After dinner, Mom and Dad would take a walk, and by the time they got back, the kitchen would be clean and the table cleared for homework, bill paying, coloring, or playing board games. Sometimes my mom would make homemade play dough. If it were Thursday, we would watch The Cosby Show and have popcorn or rocky road ice cream.

At eight o'clock, we would get tucked into our bunk beds. Our rooms were so messy that Dad would always say, "Clear a path to your bed so I can kiss you good night!" After we hopped into bed, Mom or Dad would come pray with each of us, and once in a while they would read bedtime stories. The older girls were allowed to keep their lights on while they read their own books in bed. I remember often hearing my parents popping more popcorn and laughing in the living room as I fell asleep on the top bunk. Some nights I would sneak down the hall to see if they would share a little. Sometimes they would; other times they would say, "You already brushed your teeth, get back to bed!" And I would scuttle off back to the bedroom.

LIKE MY MOM

By the time I was six, my parents both worked at home during the day, my dad worked for NASA at night. Our family had an art business: my mom painted, my dad made frames for her paintings, my sisters and I were often the subject of mom's paintings. I loved to sit in my mom's art studio and watch her paint.

In the evening, when the rest of the family would gather around the TV, I would often grab a stack of books from the shelf in my mom's art studio. I loved looking at her books about famous artists. Even as a little girl, I found Leonardo De Vinci's drawings and sketches captivating. With just a pencil and pad of paper, I would spend hours trying to copy his drawings. When my mom realized that I loved looking at her art books, she began using a black marker to draw bathing suits on the naked statues. Whenever I would come across an image that didn't have enough clothing, I would find a marker and add the clothes myself.

I loved creating things, so for every birthday and Christmas, I would ask for art supplies. My parents always encouraged my creativity and talent. I can't remember the day that I decided to be an artist like my mom, but that dream was planted before I had teeth.

From the time I was old enough to push a chair up to the kitchen counter, I wanted to be an old-fashioned homemaker, too. I began to notice that not everyone lived like we did, not all the kids had moms, dads, and sisters all in one house. Some parents wouldn't even let their kids have pets or play with paint. It made me sad that some kids had to be home alone at mealtime, eating TV dinners because their moms were at work. I began to wonder how their lives ended up that way. I wanted my kids to have a happy family like the one I was growing up in.

When I Grow Up

My home-centered childhood had a big impact on my future. I knew from early on that family life had to be created and nurtured—a happy family didn't just happen. When I thought ahead to the future, I wondered who would make my house a home if I went to work like some of the moms I knew. Who would plant the gardens? Who would teach the children to set the table? Who would make sure there was milk in every glass? Who would reorganize all the board games when the stack toppled over? Who would get the grass stains out of the little dresses? Who would put band aids on the little knees? Who would wipe the spaghetti off the baby's face? Who would have time to cuddle on the couch with the kids and read book after book? Who would have time to prepare a healthy and beautiful breakfast, lunch, and dinner? Who would play Candy Land? Who would catch a toddler at the bottom of the slide? Who would bake pies, cookies, and cinnamon rolls? Who would sew curtains and cut out coupons? Who would fill the vases with fresh flowers?

My heart told me that I would do all these things, and I would be just like my mom.

DREAMING AND DOODLING
IN MY DESK

Our home was a place of creativity, games, music, art, conversation, and activity. Life was good. I was happy. There was never a dull moment.

When I started going to school, I quickly became bored and discouraged. I didn't like sitting in desks. I didn't like playing with the other kids; they were mean. I felt confused by the worksheets. I didn't like standing in lines. I didn't like doing math problems. I didn't like spelling tests. I didn't like the sound of the teacher writing on the chalkboard. I didn't like the streaks and dust left by the chalky eraser. I didn't like the lights in the ceiling. I didn't like the noise in the cafeteria. I didn't like the way my clothing felt when I sat in my desk or played at the playground. And most of all I didn't like losing my freedom. Every minute of my life was controlled by someone else who didn't even know me.

There were a few things I did like. I liked the pencil sharpener at the front of the classroom. I liked counting the little tiles on the floor. I liked the inside of the desks. I liked the closets where we hung our jackets. I liked the little cubby under the slide at the playground, and I liked walking on the balance beam. Most of all, I liked watching the big clock in the center of the wall in the front of the classroom when the hour hand pointed to the big three. I also liked the bell that would ring at the end of the school day.

I became a daydreamer. I would doodle on my schoolwork. I would play with my pencils and make origami when the teacher wasn't looking. I would look out the window and imagine I was somewhere else. I felt like school was a waste of time, and I didn't see why I should have to go. I wasn't even good at schoolwork; the letters swirled around on the page, and long lists of math facts made me dizzy. I wanted to go home and build cities in the sand pile. The kids at school would always smash the cities at the playground.

My problems at school were creating problems at home. My report cards were an embarrassment, and the grades I brought home declared I was lazy, dumb, and immature. I was told that if I didn't try harder I would fail second grade. I didn't care about grades or failing, so my dad told me that if my next report card had no Ds, I could have a pet guinea pig. At last I had a reason to try harder in school—I desperately wanted my very own pet. I worked hard to pass second grade and somehow I made it. I showed my mom and dad my all-Cs report card, and off to the pet shop we went so I could pick out my new best friend. There were two guinea pigs for sale. I chose the one that didn't bite me and named her Nibbles.

That summer, Nibbles and I made a new friend named Amy who lived in the woods at the end of our street. Amy loved animals, nature, art, and exploring too, and she was about the same age as me. She had lots of pets, including a guinea pig, eight rabbits, a few cats, a few dogs, birds, fish, and a squirrel. She also had a tree house and a fort. We had a lot in common. We could both fit a quarter between our two front teeth, and we both liked to play Monopoly. I wanted to be a mom and an artist when I grew up. She wanted to be a model and a fashion designer. But for now, we just wanted to climb trees and catch reptiles in the woods. We quickly became best friends.

THE DREADFUL
SCHOOL PICTURES

School picture day arrived. I looked at the nine-year-old girl in the mirror. Freckles. Big ears. Big nose. Big teeth. Big gap between my two front teeth. Bad hair. Black eyebrows. I wanted to stay home. I didn't want to remember what I saw staring back at me that morning. I still had last year's school pictures hidden under my bed. I wanted to be beautiful, popular, and smart. But I felt ugly, ignored, and stupid. To make matters worse, I knew I needed glasses, too. I tried to pretend like I didn't, but I couldn't even see the chalkboard. Of all my troubles the worst thing of all was the fact that my third grade classroom had no windows. I never knew if it was windy and rainy or bright and sunny. The artificial lighting above was nothing compared to the sunshine I longed for outside. Without windows I always felt disoriented.

I didn't smile for the camera that day, and I didn't pass third grade. I still couldn't read without feeling seasick. I still hated math. I had one goal: to go home for summer vacation and pray for the school to be destroyed by a hurricane. We lived in Florida—it was possible. I wanted to be a mommy and an artist, and I couldn't see how school was going to help me live my dreams. And how could I go back to the same school again? Third grade was bad enough the first time. I didn't want to go back to school without windows. The kids would know I failed and make fun of me. I wanted to hold my guinea pig, make maps of Amy's woods at the end of the street, look at encyclopedias, and draw pictures.

If I had been born twenty years later, I suppose I would have been labeled with "dyslexia" and maybe "Asperger's Syndrome." In the right school, they may have even called me "gifted." But in the 1980s, kids like me were considered "immature" and called "daydreamers." We became failures and were required to repeat whatever grades we couldn't pass—I thought I would always be in third grade. An awkward 12-year-old boy named Victor had been in third grade twice already. He was worried that he would be stuck there forever, too.

As it turned out, a hurricane didn't hit Oak Park Elementary School in the summer of 1984, but something just as wonderful did happen. I finally learned to read! While we traveled from state to state going to art festivals during the summer, my mom often would read to us to pass the time. I loved listening to the stories. One night she was reading The Chronicles of Narnia, and just when the story was getting really exciting, my mom put the book down. I asked for one more chapter, but she said to me, "If you want to find out what happens next you will have to read it yourself."

That night, on the top bunk of our RV, I turned on my nightlight and labored over every word. I tried so hard to put the sounds together and slowly began to understand each word. The more I used my imagination, the easier it was to read. It took an hour to read just one page, but the story came to life. I wanted to know what was going to happen next, so I kept reading. Suddenly, I wasn't thinking about the letters or the words, and the words were no longer swimming around on the page. I turned to the next chapter and then the next, and before I knew it, I had finished the book on my own. The next day I didn't wait for my mom to read to me. I just asked for the next book in the series, and I read it myself.

Third grade was better the second time around. I didn't enjoy it, but I knew exactly what to expect. I had seen all the textbooks before, but this time I could read them. I still thought they were boring; I would rather have been at home reading the encyclopedias all day. The kids in my class actually looked up to me since I was a year older. And I was pleased to have a seat close to the chalkboard, the clock, and the pencil sharpener. I even had a nice teacher, Mrs. Ryland, who never stopped smiling. A teacher with a sunny disposition made up for the lack of sunshine in the classroom.

Fourth grade followed, and though I was doing well in school by then, I was happy to hear the news that our family was going to move to Ohio at the end of the summer after the art show season. My dad was asked to help plant a new church, Calvary Chapel in Cincinnati, where he would be the pastor. This was a career change for him, having lost his engineering job at NASA after the Space Shuttle Challenger explosion. I was just happy that I would be going to a school where no one knew I had failed third grade. Perhaps it would even have windows. I also was excited about the prospect of seeing snow and living in a two-story house! My sisters didn't want to leave Florida, but I couldn't wait.

SHARING A CANVAS

I loved only one thing more than watching my mother paint. It was that moment when she would bring me close enough to decipher her brush strokes and then pass me the paintbrush.

First mom would allow me to do the easy parts. Then, she would show me how to do the detail work. She let me enhance the clouds with a little sunlight, add flowers to the grass and some blue to her skies, and splash some foam onto her beaches. At first we worked together on the same sections. Gradually, she would give me my own corner of the canvas. Sometimes she would give me a canvas of my own and let me use her leftover paints. Her old paintbrushes became my greatest treasures.

For years, my family had spent the summers traveling to support my mom's art career. Even after my dad became a pastor, the local church where he served was willing to give him the summer months to travel since the small congregation could not support us financially. So it was easy for us to take to the road. Mom painted all year to prepare for these tours, and my sisters and I were always ready for an adventure. We packed up the RV with my mom's paintings and waved goodbye to our friends for a few months. We celebrated my tenth birthday at a campground, and by the end of that summer, I had visited a total of forty-seven states.

Every weekend we would set up the art display in a different city at street fairs, art shows in parks, and festivals in the town squares. My sisters and I had so much fun exploring new towns and cities and looking at all the interesting art made by the other artists. I would often see things I wanted but didn't have money to buy.

Once I saw my mom trade a small painting for a set of handmade soup bowls the artist in the next booth had made. That gave me an idea. I asked my mom if I could also have some of her small prints and paintings to trade for things made by other artists.

I discovered some beautiful little pottery boxes that would be perfect for housing my coin collection, so I returned to the booth with my mom's art, looking at the most desirable box. The box's creator smiled at me, and I got up the courage to ask if he would trade one of my mom's paintings for my favorite box. I was so nervous about this new interaction that I was amazed when he said yes. He picked out a small print, and I chose the blue box. I ran back to my mom excited to show her my beautiful treasure.

As the summer passed I traded for lots of neat things: wooden puppets, handmade puzzles, a glass jewelry box, a scarf, a pottery tea set, doll clothes, some jewelry for my mom, and Christmas gifts for my sisters. Most of the artists couldn't afford to buy art from each other, but I had discovered that they were almost always happy to trade.

THE STONE MASON
OF TERRACE PARK

The little red house that my family moved to when we first arrived in Ohio was built in the late 1700's and had served as a fisherman's cottage long ago. I loved the stone fireplace, the wooden floors, and the rocky Ohio hillside. The house had two pianos and a big front porch. Every night after dinner, we would put the food scraps outside on the back porch for the raccoon family that lived in a hollow tree. We knew that if we didn't feed them, they would dump our trash cans and spread garbage all over the yard.

Heather and I had never had our own forest or river before. So as soon as we moved in, we put on our boots and headed out into the wooded hillside. We set up a camp near the bank of the Little Miami River and began to carve trails through the ravines. Trail blazing was difficult and tedious work. We had to dig out the side of the hill and remove all the large rocks. In the process, we formed an enormous stone collection of all sizes and shapes.

My dream was to build a secret village on the hill. After school each day when everyone else was busy, I would disappear out the backdoor with my dog Rocky and build. My village consisted of stone cottages for my rabbit, turtle, and kittens, and another cottage for the wild squirrels.

I had planned on being an artist, but now I opened my mind to a new passion. Oh how I loved to build with stones. Heather and I would wash all the mud off each one and carefully examine them, marveling at their blues, greys, whites, blacks, and even yellows. We would carry our favorites back to the hill. When Heather wasn't around, the neighbor's four-year-old son would help me out with his little wagon. I loved gathering piles of stones, not knowing yet what I would build. First I had to see the stones. Then, I would imagine what they could become when I put them all together. I would make piles by sorting the different sizes, shapes, and colors.

Rocky often stayed very close, alerting us if strangers ever came near. We felt protected by his deep intimidating growl, and we never kept him on a leash. He took pleasure in scaring away strangers. I also felt like God's eyes were on us as I played. I had a feeling that He put those stones there just to see what we would do with them. I knew that God loved to make interesting things—there was evidence all around us. When I was out in nature working with my hands, I felt close to God, like I was simply doing what I was created to do.

Sometimes, my older sisters, Linda and Charity, would come with me into the woods by the river where we would skip stones—our oldest sister, Sunny, had gotten married and moved away with her husband by then. When the older sisters came along, we could take longer hikes and do things that were more dangerous. We would roll the larger stones to a shallow place by the river's edge and build dams and waterfalls. We discovered a mysterious little island not far from the shore. We spent months tossing or rolling large rocks into the river hoping to raise up a bridge of stones to it. I remember the day that the river was running low, and we were able to cross over to the island on a bridge of stones that we had made ourselves.

Rocks, stones, minerals, and gems became my special interest that year. I loved reading the encyclopedias after school and on the weekends. I especially loved the pages with pictures of all the different types of stones and minerals from around the world. My older sister had a beautiful stone called a Tiger Eye; it was like solid gold to me. My favorite exhibits in the museums were the gems and mineral exhibits. Stones of every color imaginable had been gathered from all over the world, every stone telling a story, preserving history dating back to the seven days of creation or Noah's flood. Perhaps volcanoes formed them. I could not begin to imagine the stones still hidden deep in the caves of the earth where only God could see them, yet He placed them there. With all my heart, I wanted one of every kind of stone in my collection, but I had to be content with the treasures that I collected from the streams and forests of my growing up place.

That year, my grandparents took me to a gift shop that had all kinds of rocks and shells. There were dozens of buckets, each with a different kind of stone. I didn't have a cent, but my grandmother said I could pick one. I was about to pick out a little Tiger Eye stone when my grandpa spotted a large rock up on the shelf just out of reach. He held it in his hands and told me it was really special. I looked carefully trying to find the beauty in that rock, but it was so grey and lumpy on the outside. Then, he turned it over. The rock had been cut in half, and on the inside it was full of beautiful, shimmering crystals. We looked at it together, as it glowed and shimmered, and then he placed it in my hands.

"Don't forget Sarah. It's what's inside that counts. Looks can be deceiving," he said, handing the cashier some money. The rock was mine—a gift far more precious than rubies or diamonds.

I loved to carry my geode everywhere with me. I even brought it to school, showing it to all the children I would happen to meet. First I would hold it so they could only see the grey and lumpy side, and I would say, "Look at my beautiful rock!" They would take a look and quickly lose interest or laugh at me. But then I would turn it over and show them what was on the inside. Suddenly the "Oohs and Aahs" would follow.

Sarah's Journal

The Perfect Rock

When I was twenty years old and living in Austria, I had the opportunity to do some work at a castle. There were many projects to choose from; I chose to build rock gardens and retaining walls from the stones and rocks collected and dug out of the mountainside. Sometimes I would go searching for the perfect rock, and when I found it, I would ask some of the strong guys who also were working on the grounds of the castle to help me bring it to my garden.

Sometimes I would just show them a rock and say, "I need twenty rocks about this size. Try to find round ones."

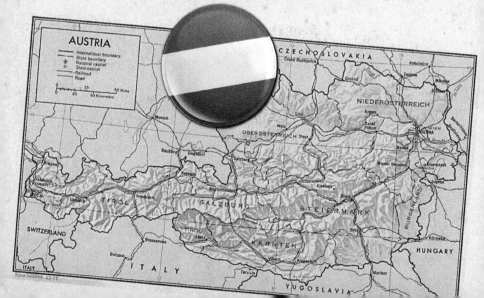

Later in my life when my husband and I traveled through the walled villages of Italy, we always enjoyed the beauty of the stonework all around: stone walkways, stone streets, and stone fireplaces. I always wondered about the people who carefully built each structure—some had been built more than a thousand years ago and were still standing, still beautiful, unchanged. I would run my hand over the cool stones and wonder where each one came from, and then I would look out over the countryside where wild streams and rugged paths twisted and turned among the hills. Scattered about were more stones. Where did they all come from?

Over the years I have enjoyed traveling to many places with stone streets, stone bridges, even castles and fortresses, and someday I know that I will be a stonemason. For now, I'm just busy raising children.

Happy Homeschooling

I really enjoyed fifth and sixth grades at my new school in Ohio. The old historic school buildings were in the center of beautiful Victorian neighborhoods. The classrooms were bright with high ceilings, wood trim and big windows. I could see the snow fall and the leaves change from my window. My little sister and I loved the walks to and from school, and often we would save our milk money for ice cream on the way home. I even had teachers who saw my artistic talent and encouraged me to add art to all my book reports and let me help decorate the classrooms.

School was no longer something I dreaded. One of my teachers started each day with a brain game or logic puzzle on the chalk board, and I was always so proud to be the first student to solve the puzzle, even though I had to wear my glasses to see the board. I had a friend or two and got into a fight or two—once a bully was making fun of my little sister and me, so I showed her my fist. She ran home crying with a bloody nose and decided to be my friend after that.

For my seventh grade year, my sisters and I were moved to a new school district—one of the "better" schools by reputation. I had always gone to small town schools before, but this middle school was one of the big city schools, and it was frightening. The fact that it had no windows didn't even compare to the behavior of rowdy boys and bullies. I was grabbed and teased. I walked into the "tattoo parlor" in the girl's bathroom, supplied with razors and permanent marker. While waiting in the lunch line, I was offered a "good" deal on any kind of drug I'd like to try. Four girls in my middle school were pregnant. And I'd often get lost in the maze of halls and stairways between classes. My report cards also suffered. There were no art classes or logic games on the blackboard, and I felt myself failing socially and academically. This may have been a normal educational experience for most American teens back in the early 90s, but it was a shocking change to me.

That same year, my mom began homeschooling Heather for health reasons. That left me waiting at the bus stop alone each morning while Heather sat at the dining room table with a pile of workbooks, a big globe, and a pack of colored pencils. And popsicles. My mom rarely forgot to hand out the popsicles. Sometimes she even sat outside under the dogwood tree to do her schoolwork or played during school hours! Homeschooling was rare back then. I hadn't heard of it before. I was jealous.

Mom started getting homeschooling magazines in the mail, and I looked through big piles of them with her, their covers adorned with families, most with a dozen or so children all in matching hand-sewn clothing. I didn't know what that was all about—I didn't want to wear homemade dresses to match my mom and sisters—but the situation was becoming harder to handle at school, and I wanted to come home and stay home. One day I came home after a very bad day at school and basically demanded to be homeschooled. I finally revealed to my parents exactly what was happening at school each day, and understandably, they were shocked. They quickly agreed that homeschooling would probably be a better option and arranged to take me out of school. So after Christmas break, I didn't go back.

My mom planned on ordering workbooks for me, but I had my own ideas of what I wanted to study. So she set me free to learn all about the things I was interested in. It didn't take long for me to fall in love with learning. My parents were serious about the math curriculum, but my interests inspired the rest of my schooling. I woke up most mornings excited to start the school day, and my family had to call me away from my studies to come help make dinner. I studied ancient Egypt for several months. I took field trips to a few museums that had Egyptian exhibits, learned how to write in hieroglyphics, and even made a model of King Tut's mummy case.

When I was tired of Egypt, I studied the history of women's clothing and had lots of fun creating my own book of fashions, beginning with fig leaves in the Garden of Eden. I remember spending hours designing Victorian dresses. My family travelled to Washington D.C. so I could view the First Ladies' Inaugural Ball Gowns exhibit. I wanted to learn to sew, so I joined 4-H and began making my own clothes—with no intent to give my family a matching set!

I also experimented with genetics through a mouse-breeding project. I collected a variety of mice, some with spots or long fur or even glossy fur. I made a deal with the local pet store to trade baby mice for store credit. My mouse, Big Mama, had about 100 babies. My goal was to breed mice until I came up with a shiny, spotted mouse with long curly fur. I wanted to name her "Taffeta." I spent hours drawing a family tree for all my mice and entered it into the county fair. I was shocked when my mouse-breeding project won first place in the county fair! For a child who had always failed in school, I was amazed that I could succeed at anything.

I'll never forget all the things I learned in that first year.

At the end of the school year, my family prepared for our annual state-by-state art fair tour. I decided to develop my own trade with hopes of selling my artwork alongside my mother's. I was tired of being poor. I never had any spending money, but I was too young to get a job. So my parents helped me start my own business selling my clay jewelry. The earrings I fashioned looked like tiny fish, dogs, and cats. People loved them. Success again! Not only did I make over $1000 in that one summer,

I also learned more math skills operating that little business than I did completing the whole year's workbooks.

One of my favorite aspects of attending the fairs was the opportunity to explore the historic neighborhoods in city centers. I was fascinated with architecture, and I would often sketch original historical homes in my spare time. It became my dream to design and build my own little cottage in the woods behind our house. My dad thought that building the cottage would be a fun homeschooling project he and I could accomplish together. By the end of the summer, I had saved up enough money from my jewelry business to begin the cottage. With my parents' help, I did the design work. Next, I built a tiny model cabin, and finally my dad and I constructed the to-scale structure together. I'll never forget the fun we had working together. I learned a lot more than math in the process. School became part of real life, and real life was a big part of my education.

THE PRINCESS
OF MONTGOMERY WOODS

There is a season, even a day, which glows brightly among my memories. It was a chilly day in early spring, and I was fourteen years old. The sunlight had found a path through the budding trees to the bare floor of my very own cabin where I sat wrapped up in a handmade patchwork quilt. My shelves were lined with canned goods and my simple pottery collection. A piece of calico fabric hung in the open doorway, and a sparrow perched quietly in the high window. I was very still and quiet so as not to frighten the little bird. The missing door didn't bother me. The opening was my way of welcoming the birds and the squirrels into my tiny home.

This was the day I would make a map of the forest. I had spent the warmer days of winter clearing trails, naming them after the turtles, chipmunks, moles, mice, baby bunnies, and raccoons I had befriended. I felt animals made more loyal friends than humans did, and they didn't seem to mind my presence or my songs. I loved my little world in the woods: my place of peace, discovery, and wonder.

The little sparrow left its perch as I began to gather all the things I would need for the adventures of the day. I placed an unmarked can into my picnic basket with a sweet potato and a pile of books to study. I didn't need a teacher, a classroom, or a school bus, because I had everything I needed in a sketchpad, pencils, and a can opener. I tied my apron around my waist and blew out the candle. Though the year was 1991, I was determined to live as if this was 1891. This was how I would learn history. "Just take your books with you into the woods!" my mother had called out when I left the house that morning. "And don't neglect your *math*!"

"Don't worry mom," I replied back, "I'll be working on my *map* most of the day!"

My path was damp with the dew of morning, and the daffodils glistened in the sun. I smiled with delight to see some of the tulips also were opening. I discovered a pattern in the stones and noticed the flowers made perfect rings under the trees. I wondered if long ago my forest had been a secret garden. I gathered sticks on the way to the clearing in the woods that I called my kitchen. The circle of rocks around my fire hole was untidy, evidence that the raccoons searched my woodland kitchen every day just after sunset. They never cleaned up their messes.

I opened up the can and dumped the contents into my cast iron pot. Green beans. I wrapped the sweet potato in a small piece of foil I had carried with me from the cabin. For a moment I was distracted by the distant sound of an old school bus passing through my neighborhood. The sound gave me chills, but I shook off the bad memories and returned to my old-fashioned world. I arranged a perfect little fire, watching the flames dance around my meal. I knew that I would need to complete my daily studies before I could take the time to draw the map of my secret world. So I laid my patchwork blanket on the ground in the clearing by the fire. After sharing breakfast with the squirrels, I laid on my back, watching the sky, working, and waiting for the day to grow warmer.

The forest was my schoolhouse. I spent the morning memorizing parts of the Constitution of the United States, and then I studied the history of women's clothing, and designed a few empire dresses that would have been fashionable early in the 19th century. I had a book of floor plans, and I dreamed of living in a house with a wide front porch and a dozen rooms, each a different world decorated with a different theme. I drew pictures of my future daughters as young women, dressing them with my pencils in silks and velvets of the medieval days. I knew that someday I would have a house full of beautiful daughters. I was hoping for seven, each one a princess with eyes the color of the ocean. I knew that their daddy would have blue eyes too. I imagined that we would meet soon, fall in love, and share a world together even more wonderful than the one I knew then.

When I finished my work, I followed the dry creek bed to my watchtower and perched in the branches of the tall prickly pine. Once I was sure I was alone, I sang like no one was listening. All the neighborhood children and my older sisters were at school, and Heather was back at the house with my parents. This was my world. Besides the creatures of the forest, there was no one who shared this imaginary place with me— no one I cared to invite in yet. My dream was too precious to share with just anyone. My heart was fragile, but my world was wild and free.

Somehow I knew I was a princess waiting to be discovered. Even my name means "princess." I had read all the stories: Rapunzel, Snow White, and Sleeping Beauty. In nearly every princess story, the lovely princess was rejected, hidden away, or lost deep in a forest. She grew up spending her days in peaceful seclusion, singing to the sparrows about her hopes and dreams and enjoying the companionship of the woodland animals. Until one day, the wind would carry her song throughout the kingdom. Only the valiant prince would follow the secret melody to discover her and her secret world, and, well . . . you know the rest.

I loved those stories, full of delights and divine intervention, a perilous journey or a furious battle, the blessing of the king, the kiss of true love, and the happily ever after. I had created an imaginary little world where I played the part of the woodland peasant, whiling away the days. But in my heart, I knew that my very own princess story would someday become reality, a tale to tell to the generations to come, beginning with my own seven daughters.

Fashion Shows, Cover Models, and Lipstick! Oh My!

I was almost fifteen years old and still playing "pioneer girl" alone in my cabin when my older sisters showed up at the door.

"Sarah! We have a great idea. Can we do your hair?" they asked enthusiastically.

I didn't understand why my sisters suddenly acknowledged my existence or why they wanted to do my hair, but I agreed to the plan. I followed them into the house and into their "beauty parlor." They had gathered make-up, curling irons, prom dresses, and all kinds of jewelry and accessories. They were acting like they had some big secret, giggling like girls do. I thought it was some kind of Queens and Orphans game, maybe rags to riches. I could see that they were trying to turn ugly little me into a princess.

I avoided looking in the mirror while they did my hair. In fact, I had stopped looking in mirrors altogether when I was about nine or ten years old. It was easy to avoid looking at myself because my eyesight was so bad that I had to be ten inches from the mirror to see myself clearly anyway. I didn't like the girl who looked back at me with buckteeth, a big nose, and a goofy smile. *She* was an embarrassment to me. I thought I was so ugly that I always looked at the ground whenever anyone was around me. I had been called so many names and teased so much by kids at school that I just stopped looking at people's faces, hoping they wouldn't see me.

I was quiet while my sisters curled my hair. It took a lot of hair spray to keep my thick bangs out of my face, the bangs I had always tried to hide behind. I didn't know much about beauty, but I did think that I needed to cover my weird black eyebrows. My sisters put lipstick on me and then made me try on their old prom dresses. I didn't realize until that moment that I was suddenly tall enough to wear them. My sisters seemed very proud of their work, telling me how pretty I looked. I had my doubts.

Once I was all dressed up, they put some film into my mom's nice camera. They had planned everything. Next they showed me how they wanted me to pose for the pictures. I gave in and did what they wanted me to do. I felt so awkward as I tried to please them. Mostly, I was just in shock that they were playing with me.

As soon as they were finished with the game, I ran into the bathroom to wash the makeup off my face. As I stood in front of the sink, I saw the reflection of a girl who could not have been me. She was someone beautiful, and she scared me. I didn't know that makeup was so powerful, so I washed it off. I thought that the weird girl with the big teeth and pointy chin would return my gaze as soon as the lipstick was gone. In my mind I was still the girl in the third grade school pictures. Astonishingly, the girl I thought I was had disappeared. A young woman was looking back at me. She was pretty, even when all the makeup was washed away.

After the photo shoot with my sisters, I began wearing my hair out of my face. I even started wearing a little lipstick. The people at church were giving me strange looks, though, so I became more determined to keep my eyes on the ground and avoid people.

A couple of months passed, and I had forgotten about the dress-up session. On a warm morning early in the summer, all three of my sisters came running through the backyard to my cabin where I was happily singing along to Michael Jackson's

"Thriller." Charity was waving a letter in her hand. "We won! We won!" They all cheered. I was confused but happy for them. I had no idea what they were talking about, but I remembered how happy I was when I won the blue ribbon for my mouse-breeding project.

"Sarah! You won the *Seventeen Magazine* Cover Model Contest! You are a finalist for the whole state of Ohio!" They pulled the letter from the envelope and read it to me. They showed me some of the photos that they had entered into the contest. The girl in the photos was pretty, but was she really me?
In addition to the bag full of makeup, accessories, and other things that teen girls love, I had won the honor of participating in a fashion show in downtown Cincinnati and ended up signing a modeling contract. Suddenly I was being whisked away to fashion shows. I was learning how to apply makeup and style hair professionally. I was modeling clothing for popular stores that I couldn't afford to shop at. I thought I was too short to be a model, but they called me "petite" and kept me busy.

During a month or two of training, I learned to look up, smile at the camera, and smile at people. I was even trained in acting and modeling for commercials. Acting came naturally for me, and I realized it was a very practical skill to have in life—it was time for me to learn to act normal. I was trained to put on the airs of a princess, to walk into the room like I was someone important, to look people in the eye and offer a firm handshake and a sweet smile. I knew what was expected of me in the modeling business, and when I followed all the rules, people respected me. It felt strange.

I also was pleased to be earning $60 per hour—a lot of money for a shy kid back in 1991. Still, the whole time I was modeling I felt like I was just pretending to be someone else. I wasn't quite sure who I was. I didn't think that the people who fussed over my clothes, makeup, and lighting would like me if they knew the real me, or at least the girl I was a few months before my sisters dressed me up like royalty and entered me into that contest.

When my sisters would bring me the newspapers and advertisements with my photos in them, the girl in high heels on the fashion page always baffled me because I continued to see myself as a quirky third grader playing dress-up. I was always so happy to get home, wash off the eye shadow, and head for the backyard where I belonged—hammering nails, setting traps, and feeding the squirrels.

MY FIRST (AND ONLY) LOVE

"Sarah? When are you going to come out of your shell?"

I looked up at Dan and Patty as they placed some books on the chair beside me just before Sunday school started. I was quiet. How could I say, *I'm happy in my shell.* I smiled shyly but said nothing. They both smiled back at me, and one of them said, "We are having a campout at our house. You are invited. There's a concert too. It will be fun."

I knew I had to go. I was the pastor's daughter and there were a few other teens coming to the church now. Everyone had expectations for me. Dan was the new youth pastor, and he was always thinking of fun things to do with us kids. This particular event was a back-to-school kick-off. I liked going to their house. They lived way out in the country, out where the stars were bright. I also loved playing with their two adorable little preschool daughters.

I had one other reason I wanted to go this time, though. I was hoping Josh would be there.

Josh and I had met in late summer at a church picnic on the lake. I was swimming with Heather and our neighbor Rebecca, who had just moved in down the street. She was pretty, smart, fun, and flirty. I was hoping that she would teach me how to be normal.

For some reason, Rebecca was really mad at me that day and hadn't said a word to me—she was giving me the silent treatment. Even though we were not on speaking terms, we were still hanging out together, hiking, swimming, and having lots of fun. She was the kind of girl who normally talks and talks; I was enjoying a little bit of quiet. The three of us were splashing around when Rebecca noticed a cute guy joining our church group on the shore.

"Does he go to your church?" Rebecca broke the silence as she started swimming to the shore.

"He's new," I answered. Though Josh lived in Indianapolis with his dad and stepmom, he and his sister visited their mom in Cincinnati on the weekends. The three of them had started coming to our church.

"He's cute," she replied. "Introduce me to him!"

She was wearing a bikini; I was wearing my dad's t-shirt with shorts. I was just happy that my friend was speaking to me again, so I agreed to make the introduction. We walked over to where Josh was standing.

"This is my friend Rebecca; she wanted to meet you," I said to him. I wanted to sink into the sand.

I stepped back shyly, feeling awkward. I felt sick as my pretty friend tried to flirt with the new guy. I was waiting for him to start drooling, but he didn't. He ignored her flirting, or maybe he didn't notice, and started talking to me instead. He talked about the baptism that had happened earlier that day and told me about his family.

After our conversation, Rebecca and I walked back to the picnic tables. I could tell that she was annoyed that he didn't notice her. But I was impressed with Josh. I'd never seen a guy ignore her flirting. And he talked to me! Rebecca and Heather decided to go hiking, and I stayed at the picnic shelter to hold a baby girl for one of the moms. A few minutes later Josh came over to where I was sitting and started making faces at tiny Rachel to get her to smile. He made me smile, too.

Then he asked if he could hold the baby. As he played with that tiny little girl, my heart flipped. I caught myself thinking, *he's going to be a good daddy someday, and I'm going to marry him.* Then, he passed the baby back to me and dashed off to talk to some of the guys. "I am going to marry him," I whispered to myself, as looked down into the peaceful face of that little baby. I looked up at Josh off in the distance.

That night, Josh filled my thoughts as I fell asleep. I dreamed we were shipwrecked on an island together, alone, and a storm was coming. He built a shelter to keep me safe. I watched and waited while he went out to gather food and firewood. We had only one blanket, so we had to share it just to stay warm. In my dream, I felt so loved, so cared for, so precious. So his. The dream seemed so real as I wrote it down in my journal the next morning.

Two weeks later on a Friday evening, my parents dropped Heather, Rebecca, and me off at the youth pastor's house for the weekend campout. When we arrived, we joined the other teens standing around the huge bonfire blazing in the backyard. We were roasting marshmallows and making s'mores when Josh showed up. I watched as he hugged his mom goodbye and joined us by the fire. He smiled. My heart melted. The moment was shattered, though, as I realized my marshmallow had caught on fire.

I was shy, but he was full of laughter. I was quiet; he was all conversation. I was contemplative; he was all happiness, always smiling. I loved the way he treated everyone with kindness and care. He was always busy helping people—cleaning up in the kitchen, carrying more wood to the fire, bringing everyone drinks.

He was everyone's friend. He even noticed and talked to me. He brought life and excitement to our quiet little group. He was such fun to be with, and when he was near, I didn't feel so shy anymore. I wasn't afraid and felt like I could be myself without being rejected. He made me feel like I had a story to tell and he wanted to hear it.

Dark clouds hid the sun the next morning as we all piled into Dan's van. We had plans to go to a Christian rock concert at a nearby park. We arrived a little early, and Josh quickly disappeared. Later I saw him working on the stage, helping the band carry equipment.

I was quite content to sit under a tree watching Josh help the guys on stage. The other kids ran off to explore the park and find something to eat. The concert began, but after a few minutes, rain started falling. I didn't know where the other kids were, and when I looked around for them, I couldn't find them. So I stayed under the big oak tree watching Josh helping the people on stage cover the equipment with tarps and plastic.

The park was nearly empty when he noticed me under the tree. "Where is everyone?" he asked. It was just the two of us. I thought it was a nice situation.

"I don't know," I confessed. "I haven't seen any of them for a while."

"Okay, stay here. I'll be right back!" he said, dashing off.

A few seconds later, he reappeared with a blue umbrella he opened over the two of us. I couldn't believe that we were sharing an umbrella. The rain was pouring down now, and we were just standing there, inches apart. I lifted my chin to look up at him while he talked to me. I have no idea what he was saying. Time stood still for a moment, and I knew that I was looking into the deep blue eyes of my future husband. I had never studied his face before—I rarely made eye contact with anyone—but here he was smiling at me and talking with me as if it were the most natural thing on earth.

Under his umbrella I was safe, sheltered, and peaceful. I felt like I had found my place on earth, but I didn't say a word. Thunder crashed, and I scooted a little closer to him. I was hoping that the rain would just keep coming down, and for the first time in my life, I was thankful for the storm. My mind wandered back to the dream I had about the island and the thunderstorm, and I had a feeling that God was smiling down on us, as if His matchmaking plan was working already. I knew that He had sent the rain.

As the day went on, I was drawn more and more to Josh's joy. I thought he was strange, in a good way. His life was full of light; he had no pride, no rudeness, no attitude, no hurry, no impatience. He was always looking to help others. Josh was playful with toddlers; he would sit on a park bench and talk with old ladies. He was part of the stage crew when he saw that the band needed help. He had no problem starting a conversation with anyone. I was fascinated by the way he interacted with people.

He also seemed to enjoy talking about God, just like he was talking about his best friend. Even though I was a pastor's daughter, I hadn't given a whole lot of thought to God up to that point. As I spent time with Josh that weekend, though, I felt like I had met someone a lot like Jesus.

Pray?

The campout didn't go as planned that night. The rain continued all evening, and we ended up playing board games in Dan and Patty's house. Well past midnight, we decided to say goodnight, but before the guys and girls went off to their separate sleeping quarters, Josh spoke up. "We should all pray together before we go to bed."

"Pray?" One of the other kids asked.

"Sure Josh, go ahead," someone else chimed in. "I guess this is a church thing."

None of us had ever thought about praying together before. The rest of us had been part of the church for years, and we expected the pastors to do all the praying. So Josh gathered everyone into a little circle, and we all closed our eyes and bowed our heads.

When Josh prayed, it was like he was talking to a close friend, someone he loved, someone who cared about him. His conversation with God was a real conversation, and his trust in God was real trust. His belief in God was his own. Josh seemed to dwell in God's love, and his heart was so full of thankfulness and confidence that God was right there and deserved his devotion. He was so thankful that God loved him and rescued him and gave him new life. When Josh prayed, God came near to the rest of us, too. I felt the love and closeness of God for the very first time in my life. I knew that the Jesus Josh was talking with was someone I wanted to know. The whole weekend I had thought I was falling in love with Josh, but I realized in that moment I was falling in love with his God at the same time.

When everyone said goodnight, the other girls had a pillow fight, but I wandered into the dark hallway to hide my tears. All I knew was that I needed to know God like Josh did. Nothing else mattered.

The next morning, we all went to church together. All the other kids scattered looking for doughnuts, but I found a seat alone in the back of the church. Josh would be playing drums with the musicians on stage during the church service. We had never had drums at church before. I sat alone watching as he set up and warmed up. I loved watching him. Sometimes I would catch his eye, and he would just smile at me like it was the most natural thing in the world. I would shyly look away.

As the musicians began the service, my heart stirred again with the longing to know the friendship of God, like Josh did. Everyone was singing all around me, and I began to listen to the words of the songs. Though I had heard them from childhood, that morning they became my own love songs to the One who gave me life. I was not normally one to cry, but a few tears rolled down my cheeks as I felt the arms of God wrap around me. I heard His whisper and felt His acceptance. I knew that I wasn't just one little forgotten speck in a great big world. I was valuable to God, and He was reaching out for me. I didn't know what to do.

I wasn't looking for God. Before that weekend, I thought I knew all I needed to know about God—I was the pastor's daughter. But I didn't know God at all. As I began to open my heart to Him, I realized that my belief in God had never been from my heart, had never been my own. Jesus had been little more than a religion, a tradition, or a story for little children. But now I felt Him holding me, loving me, calling my name, offering me His umbrella, offering me a shelter from the storm, calling me to be His princess, His beloved, His friend. As the tears rolled down my cheeks, I looked up at the cross on the wall. For the first time, it meant something to me; it spoke to me of love, real love. The songs continued, and I wanted to sing too: "In moments like these, I sing out a song, I sing out a love song to Jesus. Singing I love you Lord . . ."

When I went home that afternoon, I found my journal and began writing a letter to God. I told Him that He could have my life if He wanted it. I knew it wasn't much, but maybe He could turn it into something better. I told him I was sorry. I knew that I had been a pretender at church. I knew that I hadn't cared about the cross of Jesus. I would rather read old issues of Seventeen Magazine than the Bible. I was greedy for money and empty inside. I was selfish and vain yet full of insecurity. I saw so many weaknesses and flaws in myself.

I confessed to God that I didn't know how to be a friend—I had cared more about my pets than about people. All my life people had rejected me, and I struggled to believe that God would want me either. Rejection was painful, and in my pain, I had rejected the world and created one of my own. Before Josh offered me a spot under his blue umbrella, I thought I would be content in my forest with no need for human love. Before that day, I didn't want to be part of a church full of smiling happy people. More than once I had hidden in a storage closet on Sunday mornings when my parents thought I was in Sunday school!

I was unloving and full of fear. But oh, how I longed to be loved.

As I wrote my letter to God I asked Him to do whatever it took to make me the person that He created me to be. I told Him that I wanted to know Him, like Josh did. I didn't know what I was asking for, yet somehow I felt like I was safe under God's umbrella. He was holding me close; He was keeping me warm. He wrapped me in His love and surrounded me like a blanket. He satisfied my soul. The rain poured down and all my fears, doubts, and failures were washed away.

I knew that I would go anywhere with God. I would do anything for Him. I belonged to Him now, and I knew He would take care of me.

EMBARRASSED

No one at church knew about my modeling career. I actually was embarrassed by it, especially after giving my heart to God. Something didn't seem right, so I tried to keep it a secret. I knew I had changed. I flipped through the fashion magazines now and felt empty. When I put on my makeup and went to the photography studios, it all felt so fake. I didn't want to be fake, anymore. I wanted to be who God wanted me to be.

One afternoon just a few months after the campout, I showed up at the studio to do some modeling for a clothing line, and a good-looking young man was in the dressing room, too. Other models often were around, but usually only girls. He was friendly, but I mostly ignored him as I grabbed the clothing laid out for me, got dressed, then headed out to sit on a park bench where I had been directed.

When I got there, the same guy was already on the park bench waiting for me.

"Sarah! Meet your new boyfriend!" the photographer announced. "Just be natural, smile, laugh, have a good time." We were both modeling the latest autumn fashions, and I was terrified. In my mind, I was pleading, *please don't make me hold his hand; please don't make me kiss him!* Hiding my nervousness, I plopped down on the bench, introduced myself, smiled, laughed, and played along as he put his arm around me and gave me a little squeeze. I shyly scooted away, not sure how I could please the photographer as he clicked away.

"I like it! I like it! Shy and flirty!" the photographer said. "Perfect Sarah! Beautiful! I got it!!"

As I changed into outfit number two, I was relieved that the next shot was an independent teen fashion just for girls. I had never thought about what I would do if I was asked to wear something immodest or if I was expected to go outside of my comfort zone with another model. In real life, I had never held a boy's hand or been kissed. I wanted my first kiss to be with the one I was going to spend my life with. I didn't even want to hold another man's hand or give one ounce of my affection, passion, or heart to anyone except my future husband. And I definitely didn't want my first kiss to be with a stranger in front of a camera. I didn't know if I could do this modeling anymore. But I had signed a one-year contract. *God what am I going to do?* I cried out to God to help me and protect me.

On Sunday at church, someone showed up with a newspaper featuring one of the ads from the fall photo shoot. Everyone was surprised to see the pastor's daughter modeling the latest fashions with some guy on a park bench. My friend Rebecca told everyone, including Josh, that it was my new boyfriend. I was humiliated.

Two weeks later, I spent a Saturday working at a mall fashion show handing out samples. I was told to wear bright red lipstick, a tight black sleeveless top, a black mini skirt, black tights, and black high heels. My mom had dropped me off and planned to pick me up later that evening. By the time the event was over, my feet were hurting badly as I stood outside the mall waiting for my ride.

But when the car pulled up to get me, it wasn't my mom. It was Josh's mom. A few families and some friends from church were all going out to eat, and Josh's mom had offered to pick me up on the way. Josh's sister Becky was in the front seat, and Josh was smashed into the back seat with his drum set. Somehow, I was supposed to fit back there, too. I was very self-conscious of my short black skirt, but I didn't have any clothes to change into. I felt ashamed of who I was. What kind of girl had I become? *Was this really worth the $200 I had earned that day?* I knew what kind of guy Josh was, and I didn't think that he could share his heart and life with the kind of girl that I was dressed up as at that moment. This wasn't me.

Josh looked at me, a bit of a smile played on his lips, and his eyes were as blue as the shirt he was wearing. Eyes the color of the ocean. The chill of autumn wind was in the air as I waited for him to rearrange the drums. Then, he turned to me and said in a gentle voice, "You look really cold." He took of his jacket and wrapped it around me.

Once again I felt safe, sheltered, and warm. Loved.

High Heels
or Apron Strings?

In my teens, I started reading magazines that taught me how to be beautiful. They also explained the new American Dream to young women like me. As I curiously studied every page, I began to struggle with two drastically different concepts of what it means to be a woman in the 1990s. As I flipped through the pages of the magazines, I saw image after image of women in high heels. I read stories about the modern path for progressive women and girls, a path to become independent, smart, and sexy.

The modern woman married a career instead of a man, grew old alone, with lipstick on, of course, and had lots of boyfriends, just for fun. It didn't sound fun or romantic to me. Why, I wondered, were my dreams all about finding that one man who would love me for the rest of my life? I realized my desires were old fashioned and naive, but they were beautiful to me.

The pages of the magazines also spoke about being a woman with a mission. I wanted to be a woman with a mission, but in the magazines, that mission didn't include motherhood. The message was loud and clear that having kids and a husband was like wearing a ball and chain.

At sixteen I was trying to figure out the path I wanted to take to reach my dreams, and I knew that I wouldn't be comfortable walking down that path in high heels. I tossed that stack of magazines in the trash, and said my first "no" to the New American Dream. I wanted a life of beauty, adventure and purpose, but I would rather have a husband and children than the independent and glamorous lifestyle I read about.

As I pondered my old fashioned American Dream, I realized that one of the great things about being an American is freedom. For some women, that freedom allows them to choose a career instead of a family. For other women, they have the freedom to choose to be a stay-at-home mom. Some women have the freedom to choose both.

For me it was the freedom to hold on to my dream, apron strings and all.

THE VERSE

One little Bible verse seemed to be showing up everywhere I went: "And we know that God works all things together for good, for those who love him, and those who are called according to His purpose" (Romans 8:28). I saw it on someone's refrigerator, on a wall plaque, on a calendar, in the church bulletin, in my mom's open Bible on the coffee table highlighted. I was beginning to feel like God was trying to send me a secret message. I felt like He was saying that something was going to happen in my life that I wouldn't understand, but I could trust Him. I had heard that God talks to people through the Bible, but I hadn't read the Bible much, so it had never happened to me.

Some strange things were happening in our family during this time. One of my older sisters had just married a guy who claimed to be a Neo-Nazi Skinhead. They had an adorable new baby, but things were not going well in their marriage. Another older sister announced in December she was marrying a man who claimed to be an atheist. My parents were devastated. I was going to be in the wedding, and my mom was busy making all the dresses. They were turning out beautifully, but my mom's heart was broken. I noticed she was spending a lot of time with her Bible.

One evening in late September, we were sitting around the dining room table when my dad announced, "As soon as the wedding is over, we are moving back to California. We'll go right after Christmas." My dad was training a new pastor for our church in Ohio and planned on taking a job in California. Though I was born in California, it felt like a foreign country to me. My dad looked at Heather and me, just a family of four around the big oak table now.

"I've already lost two daughters," he said, wistfully. "You girls need to get plugged into a really good church that has more to offer to teens. We are going back to Costa Mesa where your mother and I first became Christians in the 1970s. We are going to live with your grandparents in Oregon for a while, and then we'll find a place near Costa Mesa and the beach." And that was final. No questions asked.

I left the table as soon as the meal was finished and escaped out the back door. No tears, no tears. Be strong! I said to myself as I ran barefoot through the damp grass and down the dark muddy trail. My Bible was in my little cabin in the woods. A million thoughts flooded my heart and mind of all I would leave behind. Didn't God know that my world was here in this forest? Didn't God know that my future husband was here in Ohio not California? I had just given my life to God! Why was everything going wrong?

Evening came quickly; it was a moonless night. I rummaged around in the dark until I found a candle and matches. Opening my Bible, I flipped through the pages to find the verse that I had been seeing everywhere. God must have something to say. I read Romans 8:28 over and over until I knew it by heart. What does it mean to be called according to God's purpose? I know I love Him, but what is this calling? What is God's purpose? Is this God's purpose? "Show me God what this verse means. What is my Calling?" I prayed out loud. The tears came.

I didn't return to the house until I assumed everyone had gone to bed. The cat was waiting for me by the door. I assured Sly that I would not leave him behind as I carried him off to bed with me.

THE SONG

Everything I loved was in Ohio. How could leaving be part of God's plan for my life? I had asked God for a way out of the modeling contract, but I didn't want it to happen this way!

Many friends from church came to help us pack. Even Josh and his mom came to help. I introduced him to my dog, Rocky, my pet rat, Millie, and the two cats. He drew little pictures on all the boxes he helped pack. He was all smiles and conversation. I was near tears and very quiet. I wanted to know Josh; I wanted to be his friend. I wanted to share my life, my secrets, my heart, and my future with him.

I tried to tell myself that it was just a childish crush that I should give up, let go, and find someone else in California or forget about guys altogether. *You're just fifteen!* I reminded myself. But my heart and my spirit held on relentlessly, though in silence. From the window I watched Josh carry boxes to the van, knowing and believing he was the one and there was no other. Someday, against all odds, across 2,000 miles, would he find himself loving me, too? When that day came, would he find his way back into my life? I argued with my heart, telling myself I was holding on to some fantasy, but my heart refused to listen.

A few days before Christmas, we said goodbye. The teens from church were spending a couple of days together at the youth pastor's house. We went to see the Nutcracker ballet and eat dinner out. We also went shopping at a Christian bookstore, and the pastor gave us each a gift certificate. I was in a daze and couldn't think about what I wanted, so I just grabbed a random cassette tape off of a display rack and checked out.

My heart was aching as I tried to treasure these last moments.

I didn't want to be silent and shy, so I forced myself to be more talkative and open. Josh made it easy to join the conversation. Even though we were surrounded by people, the two of us began to talk alone. Josh could see that leaving was hard for me, but he didn't know that he was the one making it so hard. I didn't tell him. In the car on the way home, he prayed for my family and me. Snow began to fall.

We all went back to a friend's house that night for a final snack. I sat down on the couch and tried not to cry. The The Sound of Music was on TV, and some of the other kids were cheerfully singing along. I couldn't. Josh's mom arrived to pick him up. She was waiting in the car, and I knew it was time to say goodbye.

But how could I? I stood by the door as Josh prepared to leave, doing a terrible job of holding back my tears. Everyone else seemed to disappear, and Josh and I were left standing in the doorway. He saw my tears and reached for me, hugging me sweetly and holding me in his arms. I melted into the warmth of his love, wanting that moment to last forever. "I'm going to miss you," he said. Then he was gone.

I grabbed my things and ran upstairs to the room in the attic where I was spending the night. I looked out the window just in time to watch Josh's car disappear into the swirling snow. I cried some more. I reached for my Bible and journal and began to read the promises of God. I wrote out my prayers and tried to find comfort and peace in God.

Did God hear me? Did He know my heart was aching? Was He really going to bring us back together someday? I reached into my bag and pulled out the cassette tape, unwrapped the plastic and removed the paper cover. Without understanding why, I was drawn immediately to the words of the last song, and began to read:

. . . Seasons changing once again. Every moment's best still one moment less we spend, together my friend. I can't hold back these tears in my eyes, this time I won't even try. Time has come and gone now we must move on. I'll admit I don't know why. Now we must say goodbye. From the lives we all leave behind we find there's much more ahead. The Father will lead us on to a better place, and I'll meet you there someday. In that time we'll see what was meant to be a special moment to cherish for all of our lives, but for now we must say goodbye. . . . White Heart

I read the words over and over, knowing that they were written for Josh and me. I was filled with faith, believing the song was a promise from God that He would lead us to a place where we could share our lives together sometime in the future. I fell asleep that night with peace. My heart was comforted knowing that our goodbye was not forever. The love I had in my heart for Josh had been planted by God, and he had plans for our future. He was the Matchmaker; He was writing our love story.

I replayed the goodbye hug in my mind a million times. I had never felt such a sense of belonging, peace, and contentment as I did that night when he wrapped his love around me. Something else happened that night too— something greater. I discovered the personal, intimate, caring, and compassionate heart of God for me. The Creator of the universe cared about me and was doing something real in my life. I felt God's nearness. I felt His arms around me and knew He would never let go. He never said goodbye, not even temporarily. I heard His promise, and understood how personal His love was, just for me.

New Beginnings

We drove across the northern states toward our new home in the dead of winter. The days stayed cold, dark, and harsh from morning until evening. We encountered snow-covered mountains, ice storms, and a wind chill that whipped through every layer, no matter how many socks I had on my feet. Mom took the opportunity to teach us about the Oregon Trail and the Pioneers. I was just happy that our journey west was in a van and not a covered wagon. Our dog, Rocky, and cat, Sly, came along. Sly stayed close to me and seemed to understand the loss we all were feeling. Even he had to leave behind his best friend, Peanuts, the kitten he grew up with.

Heather and I began to open up to each other on the trip West. We knew we were in this together. I told her about Josh and the song. And she told me to believe and never doubt, never give up hope. We were both learning to trust God, and I was thankful that my sister was becoming my closest friend. Our initial destination was Portland, Oregon, where it rained every day. My mom, Heather, and I were going to live with my grandparents while my dad went house hunting in California. I began to write letters to Josh to do my part to try to keep our friendship going. I didn't tell him about the goodbye song or that I wanted to marry him or that I thought God was going to bring us together someday. I just wrote to him about the things that were happening in my life and about the amazing things I was reading in the Bible.

My mom gave me her Bible when we moved. She got a new one for Christmas, and her old one was full of notes and highlighted verses. I started reading all the things she underlined, and I was amazed at the wonderful things I found. I was on a treasure hunt—so many promises.

We moved to California on the day that it finally stopped raining in Portland. My dad found an apartment near Calvary Chapel in Costa Mesa, the church where my mom and dad began following Jesus in the early 70s. Almost 15 years earlier at that same church, Pastor Chuck Smith held little baby me in his arms and dedicated my life to God's care, calling, and protection. My parents told me that after the dedication service, a woman came up to my mother and told her that there was something very special and unique about the prayer that the pastor prayed over my little life, and my mom had pondered her words in her heart.

I loved living in California and being close to the Pacific Ocean. I also loved being part of Calvary Chapel and learning more and more about the Bible. Surprisingly, I found I was no longer afraid of groups of people and began making close friends in the youth group. I enjoyed going to church camps, and most of all, I loved going on short-term mission trips to Mexico.

My first mission trip consisted of eight days of intense heat, hard work, dirt floors, beans and rice, beans and rice, and more beans and rice. But I'll never forget the faces of the children we met as we spent our days helping on a ranch that served as an orphanage and school for deaf and mute children.

A man named Luke welcomed us and told us the story behind the Ranch. When Luke was about five years old, he had an accident that left him half deaf. His parents thought that he would soon lose all of his hearing, so the family learned sign language. When Luke was about ten years old, his parents decided to move to Mexico with their six children and start a free school for deaf children. With a down payment of about $50, they bought a few hundred acres of land and built a two-room shelter with no walls.

Within two weeks, Luke's family had a dozen students attending their school without walls. Eventually they built a house for their family, but within months it burnt down. They were in a place of complete dependence upon God. They had lost so much, but God did not fail them. Luke told many stories of the sacrifices, trials, and heartbreaks his family experienced as they followed God's call to care for these deaf children.

I would have stayed if I could—something about being with these children filled an empty place in my heart that I hadn't known existed. I was always longing to be loved, accepted, and cared for, but I was never satisfied until I learned how to love, accept, and care for these precious little ones. They were all deaf, and we couldn't communicate, but somehow that didn't matter. I was no longer looking to be loved but to give love, and at once I began to understand the love and compassion of God.

My parents must have been surprised to meet me when I came home. I left the old Sarah in Mexico; I was someone new. I had a new perspective on life. All the things that had been important to me before Mexico seemed so trivial when I got home. Suddenly, I didn't even mind sharing a room with Heather. I even began to see my own sister as someone who needed to be loved.

My heart was no longer content with the normal American life—the materialism, the pursuit of money and entertainment, the time wasted in front of the TV. These things became distasteful to me. I wanted to go back to Mexico and get dirty if I had to, spending my days meeting the deepest needs of little children.

Something within me began to say, *I am home when I am with orphans, when I am walking on dusty streets holding dirty hands. That's when I feel God's presence the most. When I'm loving the lost, the hurting, the forgotten, or any little child, then I am loving God, and He is loving others through me.*

Heart's Closet

One Friday night, I wanted to work on an art project but couldn't find a pencil. While rummaging through my drawers, I realized that it was time to clean my room. My parents didn't even tell me to this time!

I cleaned my room like never before. I pulled everything out from under my bed. I dumped out the junk drawers. I emptied my shelves. And I finally discovered what was in the magazine holder—one Brio Magazine and lots of odds and ends.

It was like Christmas all over again except it was all mixed up with junk. I got a trash bag and started to sort all of my things into little piles. I made a pile of photos, a pile of pens and pencils, a pile of books, a pile of art supplies, one with letters and stationary, and a big pile of other people's things. Next, I gathered up a collection of boxes, buckets, and bags to organize all my things. Soon I had a big bag of trash and lots of containers overflowing with forgotten stuff and unfinished projects. I surveyed my clean room and wondered what to do with all these containers of my new things.

Around 11pm my parents popped their heads in to say goodnight and were shocked at my clean room.

"As soon as I put all these things away I'll be finished!" I told them.

I thought of the high shelf in my closet. Perfect! When I opened my closet door, I discovered that my shelf had fallen down and was now buried in clothes, trash, and more stuff! Not only was the closet a mess, but there was some weird smell that reminded me of rotting Easter eggs. So I shut the closet door, had a snack, tiptoed around all the containers of stuff, and went to bed feeling like I had a clean room, but thoughts of my closet haunted me. I knew that I had to clean out that messy closet, too, or all my little containers would soon be tipped over, all my stuff would be stepped on, and my room would be a mess again.

When morning came I didn't really feel like doing anymore cleaning, but as I read my Bible that morning I read about how Jesus makes our hearts clean. I got to work on that closet, pondering the way Jesus had cleansed my heart and life. I thought about how easy it is to try to look good on the outside while hoping that no one will look into the hidden places, the secret places of the heart and mind.

After I vacuumed my room, I let my dad take out the trash even though there were a few things in the trash bag that I didn't want to give up. Letting my dad take out the trash made it easier to let go. By Saturday afternoon, my room was clean and pretty, from deep in the closet to the desktops and windowsills. I was ready to start working on one of my unfinished art projects, so I grabbed my box of pens and pencils. Just a day ago, I couldn't find a pencil, now I had exactly 209 pens, markers, and pencils to choose from. Every color of the rainbow in one box!

Jesus sees all the hidden places. He sees all the trash. But He also sees the talents, the hopes, the abilities, and the strengths. He sees the weaknesses, fears, and troubles that we have pushed into life's corners. We need to let Jesus pull it all out into the light where we will find the treasures and see the dirt, grime, and dust. And we need to cry out like King David: "Create in me a clean heart O God!"

Summer of Silence

One Saturday the following March, my mom dropped Heather and I off for the day at Calvary Chapel. The church was hosting something called a "purity seminar." I had never heard of anything like it, and no one had ever talked to me openly about things like boyfriends, girlfriends, husbands, and wives. I had never heard about sexual purity and wasn't sure I wanted to.

By the time the conference was over that day, I knew that I didn't want to give one little nugget of my heart to anyone except the man I was going to marry. And I was pretty sure who that was going to be, although I hadn't told Josh yet. I was hoping he would be the first to bring up the subject. But now I had a new perspective about relationships. I had decided that I didn't even want to hold a guy's hand unless I knew he was the one and only.

That evening, I pondered some of the odd things one of the speakers had talked about, how the first time she kissed her husband was on their wedding day. When I was in seventh grade, some of the kids had made fun of me because I was thirteen and had never been kissed. Suddenly, I saw a kiss as something precious, something worth waiting for. But waiting for marriage? I wasn't sure.

I brought a book home with me called Passion and Purity, and my heart was awakened to the beauty of the love story between Jim and Elisabeth Elliot. In this story, Jim didn't kiss Elisabeth until they were engaged to be married. It was precious. It was powerful. I wanted a love story like that. I wanted to be cherished, adored, and held in the arms of my husband. I longed for his nearness, his kisses, and his voice. I knew that God was the creator of marriage, and His ways are perfect. I wanted to trust in Him, even with this.

Five guys at Calvary Chapel believed I was destined to fall in love with them. Running into any one of them was the worst part about going to church. It made me sad to constantly reject them, but I knew I was waiting for Josh. God had given me a promise, and someday Josh would fall in love with me.

I wrote to him faithfully every week, and I camped beside the mailbox every afternoon hoping that he would write back. I would hear from Josh about once a month, but then in the summer of 1992, the letters stopped coming. I began to doubt that I would ever see him again—perhaps our love story had been all in my imagination. Was I as ignorant and wrong about him as those five guys at church were about me?

Missing Josh became so painful that I knew I had to give up hope and let go of him. And I did. I put him into the hands of God and stopped writing to him. I stopped dreaming about him. I pushed thoughts of him out of my mind, but I couldn't stop loving him. Nothing could take his place in my heart— even tried to fill it with spiritual things, to no avail. I tried to learn to play guitar, and I tried to make new friends, but I still couldn't get him out of my heart.

At last I had a plan. I figured the only way I could fill his empty spot in my heart was to put someone else in his place. I did a lot of thinking about who that could be. I thought about all the important qualities that I would want in a husband. When I couldn't find anyone that could compare, I chose someone I felt I could admire and respect instead, someone who didn't have a girlfriend and didn't follow me around like a puppy. I wrote him a note. I felt so foolish doing it, but I just had to get Josh out of my heart.

When I went into my closet to look for an envelope, I spotted a box tucked high on a shelf covered with other boxes and folders and paper. I tugged on the box and an avalanche threatened to break loose. I jumped out of the way but not before a little book hit me in the head. I picked up the book from the floor, amazed to see my lost diary—the one with the little pink spots from Ohio! I hadn't seen it since we moved. For a moment, I forgot my task and plopped down onto my futon to bask in all the happy memories.

Day One, August 3, 1991 – the day I met Josh at a church picnic...

I began to read all the stories and the memories of the five months Josh and I shared before I moved away. The last entry was written on the night we said goodbye, including the hopeful words of that sweet song and the promise that God would bring us back together someday. Tears fell, and I let my love for my Josh fill my heart all over again. I began to cry out to God in prayer, asking the Lord to protect Josh's faith, his calling, and his purity, and to allow Josh's devotion to the Lord to grow. As I prayed, God's peace came over me, and I knew that everything was in His hands. I committed to battle for my beloved in prayer, that he would turn from temptation and never settle for less than God's best for his life.

I began to fill my journals with prayers for him, but months passed and he never wrote to me. As I wrote out my prayers, I pleaded with God to do a work in our relationship, to show me if He really wanted me to wait for Josh. I asked God for a letter from Josh, and I prayed that in the letter he would say, "I love you" three times. As I wrote the prayer down in my little book, I laughed at the impossibility of my request. Josh had never said he loved me in a letter before, and he hadn't written in five months. Once again I put him in God's hands and gave myself entirely over to God. I was at peace. I would pursue nothing further.

If there were a future for us, I would know through the answer to my prayer.

Two weeks passed. I had peacefully given up on Josh and felt no need to put anyone in his place besides Jesus. I stopped camping by the mailbox or even checking the mail at all. I was busy in the kitchen when Heather burst into the house. "Sarah! You got a letter from Josh!" she called out.

I couldn't believe her words. "Where is it?"

She looked at the mail in her hands. "I forgot it! It's still in the mail box!" she said.

We both went back to the mailbox, laughing. She was just as happy as I was to see that letter. She was the only person on earth who knew what I was going through.

I didn't open the envelope until I was alone. It had been almost six months, and I didn't know what to expect. Three letters filled the one envelope. Three beautiful, loving, heartfelt letters. Josh opened his heart to me, sharing the deeper things, and asking me to forgive him for his silence, though he didn't explain it. At the bottom of each letter, he wrote the words, "I love you." One, two, three.

I had the answer to my prayer. After that day he never stopped writing to me. Our friendship grew deeper, and with it came a longing to see each other again, wondering what God desired for us.

In January 1993, my parents announced that we were leaving California. I didn't know where we were going, but I was hoping with all my heart that it wasn't too far from Indiana, where Josh still lived with his dad and stepmother.

OF THE ST AT
CALIFO
ACT OF
L SLAT
PASSED MARCH 25
Compiled b

Sarah's Journal

Summer of Silence

Here is a prayer I wrote in my journal,
during the summer of silence:

Lord, You know my heart, You know my thoughts, and You love
me anyway. Please help me, change me, use me. Lord, You know my
future, and You know what I think is in it. You never forget Your
promises. But is this hope and promise concerning Josh really from
You? Please show me soon. I don't want to break my own heart by
believing something that is not true. Show me the truth, and now
I feel like you are speaking to my heart saying that You have
already shown me the truth and that the promise is from You.
Please don't let it be my wild imagination.

Now I lift up Joshua to You that You would draw him nearer to You each day. Protect him; give him your peace and joy. Keep him in Your word. Be the strength of his life. Guard his heart and mind and keep him pure in your sight, as You make him into the man you have called him to be. Use him and teach him, chastise him and bless him. Keep him trusting in You with all his heart.

Be his first love and don't let him put anything before you. Be the center of all his relationships, and help him to be a witness of You to everyone around him. Let your light shine through him and fill him with your Spirit.

Thank You for our friendship and keep it strong, be in the center as we help each other draw nearer to You. Keep our relationship where You want it, and help us do Your will.

Help me not to awaken love before Your timing. Help us to wait on You. Help us both to realize that only You can fill our deepest longings, fill our hearts with joy, and answer our heart's cry. Keep us on the path you have called us to walk on. Your will be done, not ours.

Give us the desires that you want us to have. Help us to seek you first, not each other, in this friendship. You, Father, are the reason we exist. You, Jesus, are the reason for our friendship; let it stay that way. In Jesus Name, Amen.

THE NAIL IN MY FOOT

Things didn't work out in California the way my parents had hoped they would. When we left, they didn't know exactly where we should go next. We stopped in Arkansas where my grandparents were celebrating their 50th wedding anniversary. Not only did we go to their party, we moved in. My Nana and Pipi owned a campground and a beer store. They had an extra trailer home on one of the campsites, so the four of us moved in.

The plan was to stay there, mow the grass for my grandparents, and figure out what to do next. It didn't take Heather and I long to figure out what to do next, with 40 acres of lakes, streams, springs, hills, and forest. We started exploring immediately. We found an island in the center of a stream, so of course we wanted to build a bridge to it.

Our family didn't bring much with us from California, just my dad's huge book collection, a case of Bible study tapes, a couple of guitars, art supplies, Sly, the cat, and the necessities. I spent a lot of time writing letters and trying to learn how to play the guitar. We were still homeschooling and did most of our schoolwork at the picnic tables, as far as possible from the beer store. My pretty sister and I didn't enjoy the smiles and winks we would get from the good ole boys.

I started reading my dad's books and listening to the Bible study tapes. My favorite Bible teacher quickly became Jon Courson. I listened intently to dozens of the fascinating talks he had recorded about following God and understanding the Bible. One talk that really stirred me was about the suffering of Christ. My heart was touched, and I prayed that I would be able to understand more of what Jesus did for me at the cross.

One afternoon while building our bridge, Heather and I found a pile of old construction scraps and carried them into the woods. Some of the boards were nailed together, so we worked hard to pry them apart. I was stomping down on an old board when I felt a piercing pain shoot through my foot. My foot was attached to the board, and a nail was driven through my shoe and all the way through my foot. I had never felt such terrible pain, as I pulled and twisted my foot in effort to be free from the long rusty nail. My blood dripped all over the board, and as I limped home, the blood formed a trail in the grass.

My parents immediately drove me to the doctor's office for cleaning, antibiotics, and a tetanus shot. I was in bad shape and couldn't walk on that foot for two weeks. I spent a lot of time on the couch writing letters to Josh, thinking about the suffering Jesus went through on the cross, and reading books from my dad's collection. *God's Smuggler to China*, *The Hiding Place*, and *Peace Child* became life-changing favorites. All three were stories of people who surrendered everything to live out God's amazing plan for them. These missionaries had loved others and brought truth, hope, light, redemption, and God's words into some of the darkest places and situations on the earth. The books contained stories of war, danger, and courage. My spirit wanted to follow the same calling, but fear and uncertainty pulled on my heart.

Something in me desired a peaceful, comfortable life. Something else told me that I was created for a mission, a calling, and a purpose on this earth. Would I accept the mission? I was afraid of what God might ask of me if I opened my heart to the call I was hearing in my spirit. I wanted so much to live a life that would have a lasting impact on the world, but I was afraid of the cost. I was afraid of what I would have to give up, of where I would have to go, of the hard work, the perseverance, the trials. Would it be worth it? A deep desire stirred in me, to set out on a mission. I didn't know how, when, where, but I knew Jesus, and I was becoming more willing to do anything for Him. After feeling just one nail in one foot for one minute, my heart wept for what Jesus went through for me at the cross. He gave His life and suffered for me, to bring hope, life, forgiveness, and everlasting love to me. He was tortured, beaten, and killed to pay the price of my soul and give me everlasting life.

After I recovered from the nail in my foot, I joined my neighbors for a trip into the Ozarks. As I played behind the waterfall, collected stones in the stream, explored the valley and followed the trail higher and higher, my thoughts were somewhere else. I was still pondering that beckoning call. I wanted to live for Him, but I was afraid. I knew he was calling me deeper, farther, nearer, and higher.

Bridge or Mountain

I am standing on a bridge between two mountains; below me are the rushing rapids. Water is crashing down into the valley from the pristine waterfall. But I am silent. I can hear a call in my heart.
I know the familiar voice of my Creator.

The sun is warm and high in the noonday sky. Water is all around me, dripping, splashing, misting, crashing, and rushing below and before me. Yet on the bridge, I am nearly dry now except for the wet mist hanging in the air. Across the bridge, a trail winds upward into the rocky mountainside. It is a treacherous path to a place of amazing views. The way is challenging, the path is narrow, and the trail is more like a climb.

In the opposite direction is the path by which I came. It is a level path that guides the travelers' feet back into the green valley. I look down the path beneath the canopy of trees, along the edge of the rushing waters, along the mountain's edge. The valley path winds through the rocks to a narrow cavern behind the waterfall where the way is slick, and with just a slip, the falling water drenches to the skin.

Now I must decide, will I turn back to the path that leads me behind the waterfall, or do I want to see the waterfall from the mountain high above? I pause here on this bridge knowing that I can't stay here long looking from the mountain to the waterfall. I like this bridge—it feels safe, and right now I would rather enjoy the view than be part of it.

But bridges are made for crossing.

I look back to the waterfall. I remember the heat of the day and the coolness of the water, with the "brrrrr" and the shiver that came over me as I splashed through the falling spring of water. The path in the valley was slippery but even children played behind the falls. I didn't come here to play in the valley. It is time to cross this bridge to the path that winds upward into the mountain.

"God?" I ask. "What is there at the end of the mountain trail? What waits for me there?"

I look over the valley, safe, warm, green.

"Most people are content to stay in the valley," I whisper, not expecting an answer. "Why are you calling me to the top of this rugged mountain?"

A gentle voice echoes in my heart "To see the villages below."
"What will I see Lord?" I whisper.

"Fields, farms, hills, mountains, rivers, and forests. My world. My creation. Your home. Your villages. Your towns. My promises. My faithfulness. Your courage. Your mission. My strength. Your efforts. My blessing. Your footsteps. My paths. Your treasures. My gifts. Your songs. My worship. Your works. My calling. My delight. Your pleasure. An earthly kingdom. A heavenly plan. Your vision. My view."
And so I cross the bridge.

PART 2

FINDING LOVE

A Hand to Hold

A letter arrived in my grandpa's mailbox, and he delivered it to me with a smile. With laughter in his voice he said, "It looks like you got a letter from Jesus Christ Himself!"

He handed me the letter. It was from Josh, but a message to the mail carrier was written on the back. He had written out a Bible verse—John 3:16: "For God so loved the World that He gave His only begotten Son, that whoever believed in Him shall not perish but have everlasting life." He had also written out the Sinner's Prayer on the back of the envelope. I laughed too. Josh didn't want to miss an opportunity to share the good news of Heaven with anyone.

Many seasons had passed since Josh and I had been together. When we said goodbye, we were barely friends. We had become very close over the past year and a half, and lately, Josh's letters were always signed with the words "I Love You." Like the others he had written, this letter filled my heart with the hope of seeing him again. He told me that his church has a campout every summer during the week of July 4th. He asked if there was any way I could come.

Though it was only a 12-hour drive away now, I knew I would have to talk to my parents. First, I prayed. Then, when my parents looked at their calendar of art festivals for the summer, the timing was perfect. They were already planning to be in Cincinnati for the Summer Fair Art Festival, and Josh's mom lived in Cincinnati. If I could get a ride to Indianapolis with her, then I could go to the campout. As it turned out, Josh's mom was going to Indianapolis that weekend anyway to pick up Becky, Josh's younger sister, and she agreed to give me a ride. Seeing Josh again was becoming a reality.

Many things happened that week in July 1993 when we finally were reunited, some far too precious to add to the pages of this book. Though we didn't even kiss, our love transformed from a sweet long distance friendship to a beautiful, vibrant, pure love. We both knew that God was at work, drawing us into a deeper relationship with Him and each other. We both knew, though we didn't say it, that we were created for each other, for a lifetime, for one mission, one calling, and one future together. One evening, we stood by the door of the church waiting for the storm to pass, watching the rain fall as lightning flashed in the distance. A grey darkness filled the world around us. A ray of light broke through, then another. Soon the rain stopped falling. We looked up, and in the midst of the darkest cloud, we saw a rainbow, as if God set it there as a sign to us of His faithfulness and unfailing promises.

Patches of blue sky began to show in the sky just as the sun began to set, lining the edges of the clouds with radiant light. We watched another storm cloud grow. The sun made the cloud glow with a soft peach. Through the silhouetted branches of the trees, we saw the bright colors of sunset. Josh first noticed the figure of a bird soaring above us, though truly it was a cloud cleverly shaped by the fingers of God—like an eagle spreading its feathered wings flying toward the sunset. The bird was suddenly changed into a swordfish, each tiny scale so perfectly in place, and then the fish took the form of a sparrow. The sparrow became a sea turtle. The sea turtle turned into a dinosaur, and then the cloud disappeared, as all the clouds above us parted to reveal the royal blue of the darkening sky. We gazed into the heavens as each new star left its hiding place to bring a fleck of light into the darkness. The fireflies of the forest began to flash their lights all around us. As we looked up into the changing sky and thought about the passing evening, we could feel God's presence. The heavens declared the glory of God who knew the number of the stars and named every one.

"See that star? The bright one on the handle of that little dipper?" Josh whispered to me. "I'm giving you that one, so whenever we are apart, you can look up into the same sky that is above us both wherever we go, see that star, and remember me. And I'll remember you."

The Sunday church service was going to be held outside the following morning. Josh was going to be playing drums. After the Saturday evening Bible Study the night before, he needed to get his drum set ready for the worship service. He would be playing with the praise team the next day and needed a screwdriver to disassemble the drums. I walked with him to the office building on the other side of camp. As we passed the pond, the brilliant moonlight was dancing on the water. We both noticed it at the same moment and looked up to see the full moon rising above the water.

We stood there amazed at the beauty around us and couldn't say a word. I felt God blessing us, beyond all we could have imagined. I looked up at Josh, wanting to be in his arms at that moment, when he whispered to me and drew me close. A frog nearby began to croak, and I laughed.

Later that night, we joined the other campers by the fire. Josh found a stick that could roast a dozen marshmallows at once. Together we made s'mores for all the people who were busy getting everything set up for the next day's outdoor service. After we were full, and all the chocolate and graham crackers had been served, Josh told me that he wanted to show me something.

We walked through a field of tall grass to a little clearing surrounded by trees. Beneath the moonlight glowed a tiny graveyard that had been unused for a hundred years. Moonlight played on the gravestones, casting light and causing the stones to radiate an eerie blue. The engraved words were shadowed with blackness. We tried to read some of the names and dates and wondered about the lives of the people whose names were written there.

We left the cemetery and followed a gravel path to the main road where we walked and talked, avoiding the puddles that had gathered the waters of the passing storm. Like a mirror, the still water reflected the sky, the trees, and the moonlight. We made our way back to the campfire and passed the pond again, enjoying the calm and quiet night. We had no flashlight, but as Josh opened his Bible, the firelight and moon's glow illuminated the pages, and he began to read to me from Isaiah 53, how Jesus came not just as a shepherd but as the Lamb of God.

"He was sacrificed for our sins and wounded for our transgressions. He was bruised for our iniquities, and the chastisement for our peace was upon Him. By His stripes we are healed."

On a night like that where everything was so beautiful and so right, it was easy to love. Yet we were reading about real love that is proven by the sacrifices it makes for its beloved. Jesus, the source of our love, was beaten, hung on a cross, and killed for us. "Greater love," Josh read to me, "has no one than this, but to lay down one's life for his friends."

We watched the fire, both thinking of how God had brought us to this day, to this place, and filled us with His love. The beauty and wonder of His creation was displayed all around us, magnified by the joy of sharing the night with him. I looked at Josh, as he watched the embers sparkling below the flames. The firelight cast a shadow of my profile on his cheek. I treasured the moment that I was near enough to see him there in my shadow. I watched his lips as he began to pray. At first he took my hand, and then he put his arm around me. I rested my head on his shoulder. We poured our hearts out to God; what more could we do? We thanked Him for the storm, and all that came after it. We put the future into His hands and asked Him for His plans for our lives. We prayed for a long time, and then we said goodnight.

I went to my tent and climbed into my sleeping bag. Before I fell asleep, I looked out the window toward the fading fire. I watched as Josh returned to the fire with his Bible, seeking God alone. The Creator of the universe had called to him to come, and he was listening. The Creator of the Universe was drawing Josh into His presence, and he responded, ready to listen, ready to hear His heart and obey His voice.

FOOTPRINTS

After Josh and I said goodbye in July, my family returned to Arkansas, packed up our few belongings, and drove to Florida. My mom had some art shows scheduled, and we spent a couple of weeks living at a campground, homeless. Or you could say we were "in-between houses." The first art show did not go well, and we began to wonder how long we would remain unsettled. I was enjoying living in a tent on the Gulf Coast of Florida, surrounded by the beauty of nature, feeling close to the heart of God. The second art show wasn't going well either, until the mayor of the city showed up and bought several paintings. An hour later, several council members and friends of the mayor wanted to buy my mom's paintings, too.

A week later we were renting a beautiful home in Bethune Beach, Florida. The house was a block from the ocean and had a big deck on top of the roof with a beautiful view of the ocean and the Intercostal Waterway. I had nothing to do but study, paint canvasses, bake bread, and walk on the beach with my sister or with God—two of my closest friends.

I would often walk along the ocean's edge for hours at a time, collecting shells while pondering life's big questions. I didn't know where I was headed as I felt my childhood rushing out with the tide. I was seventeen. All my dreams were the same as they had been since I was a little girl—I just wanted to be a mother and an artist. In the past couple of years, I added just two more things to my list: I wanted to be Josh's wife, and I wanted to answer God's call upon my life to serve as a missionary in foreign countries. All my dreams seemed so far off as I tossed dying starfish back into the sea, giving them one last hope.

One day as I walked, I noticed my footprints would fill with water behind me, reflecting the colors of the sky. I remembered the puddles left after the storm when Josh and I were together the summer before. Then, the next wave would come, and my footprints would be gone forever. Yet as long as I kept walking, I was always making more footprints. As I walked along, I knew I wasn't really alone. I was aware that God—the Creator of the ocean and the beach and the sky—was with me on those walks. I sensed that He enjoyed those days as much as I did.

In those hours near the water, all the troubles of life and worries of tomorrow seemed to wash away. It was just God and I. I would wait, I would watch, I would remember, and I would listen. When my heart was quiet, after all my thoughts were poured out like prayers into the sea, I would hear Him. I would see His beauty in the colors of the sky. I would feel His power in the surging waves. I would find His wisdom in the changing tides. I would discover His creativity in the clouds. I felt God's purity in the wind, as I thanked Him for the sweet innocence of the love He brought to Josh and me, as we learned to treasure each other as gifts from God. The seagulls would soar above and dive into the sea, and I would cast my heart into the ocean of God's love, His grace, His calling. He was always beckoning me to a deeper place of surrender to His love, to His heart, to His voice.

Those days were all about promises, dreams, and plans, and they were filled with prayers, songs, and visions. I would often check the mailbox on my way to the beach, and if I found a letter from Josh, I would wait to read it as I walked along the water's edge, always wishing he could walk beside me, hold my hand, and talk with me again. I missed him so much even though I knew I would one day be his.

Hopes, memories, whispered prayers, and quenchless longing filled many of my wandering thoughts. His sweet smile played over again in my thoughts, and so did the times when I had held his hand, when we had walked together. I thought about how it felt to rest my head on his shoulder as we watched the campfire burn out. I watched many sunsets as I walked along Bethune Beach, and as the night would fall, I would look into the night sky to find the star that my Joshua had given to me.

As the months passed, we both knew that we had to be content to wait and pray. I would bring my Bible along with me on my walks, and I would stop and read the same chapter I knew Josh was reading that day. Though we couldn't see each other or even talk, we could both listen to God as we read the same words from the Bible. I wanted so much to make footprints together, as I looked to the north and wondered when he would be with me.

When Spring Break of 1994 came, Josh showed up on my doorstep. He caught a ride with a friend of his who was traveling to Florida for a week. He took my hand, much to my dad's surprise, and we walked to the beach together.

We sat on a rock watching the waves, and I just rested in his arms as the hours passed, comforted in his love. We talked about how amazing it was just to be alive, to be loved, to have purpose, to belong to God and to each other. We pondered together the mystery that life exists at all, and our hearts were overwhelmed with thankfulness as the sun blended our two shadows into one, a foreshadowing of what was to come.

We saw many falling stars dash across the moonless sky and plunge down as if to crash into the ocean during that week. We watched the whales dive among the waves; we saw the dolphins play in the lagoon on the other side of the island. Sometimes we stayed up so late that we drifted off to sleep on the sandy shore to the lullaby of crashing waves, only to be awakened by the coming tide or my dad who happened to be taking a walk. We both knew that my parents and little sister were always around, keeping an eye on us. We didn't mind.

Josh enjoyed getting to know my family during the visit. My parents told us that they trusted us and knew that we both wanted to please the Lord. My mom and dad had some talks with Josh and me about their expectations, and then they gave us a lot of freedom to spend time together, more freedom than we would ever imagine giving to our own teen daughters in the future! We were thankful for the freedom to get to know each other after so many months and even years of separation. We treasured the days and grew in our love for each other.

One evening, as we sat on the shore watching the waves, Josh opened his Bible again, inviting God's presence into our lives and relationship. He read from Psalm 139: "How precious are your thoughts toward me, oh God. How great the sum of them. If I were to count them they would be more in number than the sand . . . " He reached for a handful of sand, and like an hourglass, released it slowly into my hand as we imagined the countless thoughts of God toward us. Then we brushed off the sand, took each other's hand, and kept walking. The colors of day changed to the colors of night, and the stars filled the sky, reminding us of how small we really were.

Just spending time together by this mighty ocean turned our hearts forever to the things of eternity. For our lives on earth are like footsteps by the sea, and this is our tide, this is our sunrise, this is our sunset, this is our starry sky—if only just for a moment. I wanted each step that Josh and I took together in this world to leave an imprint of eternity, to make an impression on this earth that will capture just a puddle of God's wonder and reflect the beauty of His glory.

THE SUNSHINE STATE

1845

Footprints

There is a smile lighting up the sky,
There is a heartbeat pulsing in the sea.
There is a breath of life, blowing through the trees
The colors of Your beauty are surrounding him and me.

We hear Your voice as You call forth the day
You kneel to the ground to touch the clay.
The clouds are gone and light breaks through the grey,
From the dirt, to life, humanity is made.

Who calls the light and darkness?
Who brings forth the wind?
Who forms the clouds and paints the sky?
Who calls His children friends?

Who calls each star by name?
Who made the way by which we came?
Who counts these grains of sand?
And holds the worlds in His hand?

FLORIDA

GEORGIA

1 Jacksonville
2 Miami
3 Tampa
★ Tallahassee
○ St. Augustine
◇ Key West
▣ Palm Beach

Time and beauty, wisdom and sight,
Gravity, pleasure, thought, and life.
Each concept Yours, perfect and right,
Before You said, "Let there be light."

In the shadow of Your throne,
Among the flowers and the stones,
Your great creation now becomes
A sanctuary of our own.

You cast your light, a shadow falls,
As two lives become one.
You breathe Your life into us both,
New life has begun.

The tide goes out, the tide comes in,
The years like sunset pass
He holds me close and treasures me,
As You hold us in Your grasp.

I see Your smile lighting up his eyes,
Your heart, in his, pulsing now for me.
And we know what was meant to be
As Your promise covers him and me.

EIGHTEEN

On July 30, 1994, I turned 18. Heather and I were visiting Josh's family on my birthday. Josh and I stayed up until midnight on my last day as a 17 year old. When my first moment as an adult began, I was with him.

It was a star-filled night as he read the Bible to me in his backyard. I wondered what the year ahead would hold as he read the first chapter of Isaiah to me. My heart filled with peace and wonder at these words: "If you are willing and obedient you shall eat the good of the land." I felt that the Lord had given me this verse to hold onto for that year and the coming years. I had such a strong desire to serve the Lord with Josh, even without knowing how God would call us to serve him in the future. I knew that we were walking in His calling, and it was my prayer that we would always remain in His perfect will.

Earlier that morning had been filled with housework. We girls wore green facial mud masks as we worked. The day started off with some bad news from Josh's stepmom, Kathy. "Apparently someone left the freezer door open, and then someone shut it after everything thawed out," she announced. "Only God knows how many chickens are frozen back together in a solid block of blood and ice."

After helping with the freezer, Josh and I went outside to enjoy the beautiful birthday weather, and he read another chapter to me from the book of Isaiah. Then more bad news. A computer at Josh's dad's office broke, and soon we were off to fix it. Josh had become the computer repair tech at his dad's office.

When we came home again, it was time for me to open presents. Josh's dad got me a Kit-Kat Clock—its eyes and tail twitching back and forth with every passing second. Heather gave me two treasures: a heart shaped locket and a blank book with little notes in it. Josh gave me a scrapbook, and we got right to work filling the first few pages with photos, memories, and art. I looked forward to filling all the blank pages with our story. I imagined that someday we would be looking at that scrapbook with our own kids.

At five o'clock I started to get ready for the surprise evening that Josh had planned. His dad turned on the 1940s music and started to dance around the room as Kathy put curlers in my hair. Heather worked on getting me all fixed-up, as she ironed my flowered dress and helped with my hair. I wore Kathy's cream-colored shoes, "diamond" earrings, and the locket Heather had given me. I was growing up. I was ready to move off into my own life, and in the midst of all the joy, I could feel a sadness stirring in my little sister. We both knew that soon she would be an only child, and I would be going my own way. We talked about the changes and tried to push the sad feelings away.

Josh arrived, all dressed up, too. He told me I looked beautiful. Heather took pictures.

With no clue where he was taking me, I got into the car and we left. We borrowed his dad's Volvo and ended up in downtown Indianapolis, parking on the fourth floor of a parking garage. We walked to the Old Spaghetti Factory, and during the 45-minute wait, we went outside, and I drew pictures of the people milling around.

Dinner was wonderful, and afterwards, we went to Union Station for dessert. We had Hawaiian Ice—kiwi, mango, and black cherry flavored. After exploring the station, we went back to the parking garage and had a hard time finding the car. But the view was amazing. Josh put his arms around me as we looked out over the city streets and watched a jazz band playing below us.

Josh still had one more place to take me. When I saw the air traffic control tower and the runway all aglow with blue, white and red lights, I knew I was looking out over his dream to be a pilot. We got out of the car, and I watched as an airplane landed on one of the distant runways. When I turned around, Josh was there holding out a beautiful bouquet of roses and lilies for me. We both were smiling. It was the first time anyone gave me flowers. I was watching all my girlish dreams come true, and then he hugged me as a plane landed just a few feet away. I barely noticed it as he held me. I would have kissed him, but we knew that the kisses must wait for another day, a day that included an engagement ring and a promise.

I tossed Kathy's shoes into the car as he took my hand. We ran together down a grassy path by the flashing runway lights. As he held my hand, I knew he also was holding my heart. We talked about sharing a life of adventure and faith, about following God, unsure of where He would lead us. We agreed that we would go wherever He called, giving up everything to live for Him, willing and obedient, just like the verse in Isaiah. Josh told me that he didn't want to live the kind of affluent lifestyle that his parents pursued but that God was calling us to a life of freedom to serve Him, free to do God's will, free to take hold of any opportunities God would give us. As he spoke, I was assured that it really was our heart's desire to live a life set apart for God's eternal purpose.

We got back to Josh's house that night just after 11 to find a box of chocolates from Josh's brother and a homemade card that read "#1 Candidate for Sister-in-Law," with a seal of approval. Heather joined us, and we spent the next hour working on the scrapbook together.

SEND ME?

On Sunday morning, Josh and I went to church together. Before the service started, we took some time to sit outside and read more of Isaiah together. My heart began to beat harder as he read the words, "Also I heard the voice of the Lord saying: Whom shall I send and who will go for Us? Then I said 'Here I am, send me.' And He said 'Go.'"

My heart silently cried out, "Lord, here I am send me!"

We sat in church together as a guest speaker shared a message that echoed all the things that we had been feeling as God moved in our own hearts. George Markey, a missionary and pastor from Kiev, Ukraine, spoke about resting in God, living totally for Him, doing God's will, and following His calling. He told the story of how he felt that God was calling him to Ukraine. He had been afraid that his wife and eight children would not be in favor of following the Lord to the ends of the earth. When he told his wife about his calling, he found out that the Lord had also put the same desire in her heart, and so they went, and all the children willingly came along.

As Pastor Markey spoke, I knew that God desired to send me, too, and He was giving me a strong desire to go to the mission field. I listened as the missionary spoke of being in a place of making life-changing decisions. "Are you going to choose to live by faith and live for Jesus, or will you go on living a fruitless life?" he challenged.

I was quiet after the church service. I wanted to tell Josh what I was feeling, and I was hoping that he was feeling the calling, too. He didn't say anything at all for a while, and I was beginning to worry that he didn't share this calling to missions that I felt. I only knew that God wanted to send me, and I was quiet. As soon as I got a chance to be alone, I opened the blank journal Heather had given me for my birthday, and I committed these words to paper:

I am willing to receive all that you have for me. Show me hearts that bleed, I see a need. Let your voice be heard in me that others may come and believe. Send me Jesus, I will go, to shine your light and let them know. Lord I desire to be part of your plan, even if the way is hard, even if I do not understand, even if I must go alone. I will be with you forever in your eternal home.

Lord, I am willing to receive all that you have for me. All the things of this world are things I do not need. I will go your way, any way you lead. No matter what the cost, let me meet the need of the souls that are lost, and of the hearts that bleed. I will give up everything for You. I'll seek your kingdom first, Jesus I love you. I want to live for You; use me, I am Yours.

A couple days later, Josh and I decided to spend time alone with God instead of spending time together. When we got back together later, we both wanted to share the things we were learning in the Bible. Out of nowhere he said to me, "If God called me to Kiev, I'd go." And I said, "I'd go too."

We took a walk to a playground in his neighborhood, both feeling God stirring our hearts. An hour passed as we prayed together. We prayed about serving God wholeheartedly, not comprising. We wanted to be a good example, not even having the appearance of anything ungodly—even when we thought it didn't matter. We asked for the overflowing of God's Spirit in our lives. Josh prayed that God would go beyond our list of possible plans for our future and do something greater. He prayed that we would be an example to believers and also to those who do not know Jesus, examples in love, in faith, and in purity.

As we prayed, we realized that we were praying to the same God that Abraham, Isaac and Moses prayed to.

THE BLESSING

When my parents came to pick up Heather and me after my lengthy birthday visit in Indianapolis, my mom and dad spent Friday evening with us at Josh's house. We had ice cream together, and all laughed at how everything in the family's refrigerator was fat-free, and yet there were eight boxes of ice cream in the freezer. We all enjoyed looking at my new scrapbook together and had a wonderful time. My parents gave Josh and me a letter that they had written for us to read together. When we had some time alone, Josh read the letter out loud to me:

Dear Sarah and Josh,

How we praise the Lord that your relationship has grown from a deep friendship into a pure and holy love. We couldn't imagine a better way for love to develop. To know that you are both being used by the Lord in one another's lives to bring you both closer to Him is so right. We pray that you are always a blessing to one another spiritually—then everything else will fall into place, because the Spirit is in charge.

Dad and I have talked to each other about your relationship for over a year, but we didn't want to push you, get ahead of the Lord, or be an artificial influence on your friendship—so we tried to keep quiet, pray for you, and give your love an opportunity to grow in the Lord. We intend to continue on the same course.

Josh, you are a really neat person, but we don't want to go beyond encouragement to ego building. We admire your commitment to the Lord, and we are so impressed by how highly your father thinks of you. When he talks about you, he reminds us of ourselves talking about Sarah. We all feel so incredibly blessed to be the parents of such dedicated kids—that our children would have such a love for Jesus and a deep desire to be pleasing to God above everything else.

Our deepest prayers are answered in you both and you really make us see and feel the truth of 3 John 1:14. We really appreciate how God seems to build people and prepare them to use their natural personalities, talents, and brains—and then brings them together. But we also know that God's plans are beyond our comprehension. We rejoice with you and love you both.

Always,

Mom

P.S. Just a personal note – Josh, it's hard to let go of my girls. But I know that the Lord is in control. When you are a father you will understand. – Dennis

INNOCENT LOVE

We sat together at the playground near Josh's house one more time before I left. Josh was quiet. Something was on his mind. Then he spoke up. He shared with me how precious it was that he would be the only man that I would ever kiss. But I could see sadness in his eyes when he asked me if it hurt to know that he had kissed other girls, even though it was back in middle school.

I looked at him, then felt his arms around me; his pure love surrounded me with strength. I knew he would never want to do anything to hurt me. He treasured me the way God intended for a man to love a woman. He loved me with a holy love that kept him from compromising my purity or taking away my innocence. So many times he longed to kiss me— and more, but God had called us to wait. He was content to love me by giving instead of taking.

I was quiet for a while. "No," I finally said. "No, because I know that I will be the only one for the rest of our lives together. But at the same time I do hurt for you because you don't know what it's like to have your hand held for the first time in your life by the one you are going to marry. But I know that I am the first and only one you will ever love as you love me, and no other love here on earth compares to this."

We wanted so much to give ourselves completely to each other; our love was becoming harder to contain. Yet we knew that it would be three more years until our wedding day, and we knew that God had called us to wait for the right time in our life to enjoy the intimate love created for a husband and wife. Josh's willingness to wait for me, to wait for marriage, and to obey the voice and word of God was proof to me of the power of God in him. I was falling deeper and deeper in love with him. If he was so faithful to me now, I had no doubt of the faithfulness he would bring into our future marriage.

Josh had his Bible and began to read to me from 2 Corinthians 11:22-23 about Paul's suffering, afflictions, trials, struggles, journeys, perils, labors, beatings, shipwrecks, and persecution. All for the sake of the call. Josh said, "I want to be like Paul."

I couldn't contain my shock that Josh would want all those awful things that Paul went through. How could he say so sincerely that he wanted to be like him? Josh saw my surprise and explained to me that he wanted to have the same kind of dedication to God's calling that Paul did. Josh was willing to suffer for Jesus' sake, to live or die, to leave all this world's treasures behind, and to give all he has to follow Jesus. Josh knew he was weak in his own strength, but he longed to reach beyond his own wisdom, power, endurance, and ability to do God's will and not his own. He wanted to satisfy the desires of God's heart and not the desires of his own heart, mind, or body.

"We are called to live for God's glory," Josh explained, "even to our own shame. Even if we must suffer for His sake. We are called to praise him. We are called to love him, even though the world hates us. We are called to serve Him. We are called the children of God, heirs of the promise. It's a labor of love. It is an honor. It is our calling. In doing God's will our joy will be full."

TO SURRENDER ALL

I was planning to head to college when our usual art fair tour around the Midwest ended late that summer. Everyone expected me to go, which was the main reason I was going. I hadn't even really prayed about it, but college seemed like the obvious next step. I had been accepted into a graphic design major at a Christian college in northern Florida and would be specializing in creating curriculum and designing textbooks for Christian schools. I had earned a complete scholarship for the four-year degree. I was planning to be a stay-at-home mom and a curriculum designer in my spare time. I had studied child development on my own for years, and I loved writing, illustrating, and teaching children. The degree would be the ticket to my dreams, and I didn't have anything else to do while Josh was going to college to be an airline pilot. I secretly hoped he would trade that dream someday for a new dream from God to serve as a missionary pilot. He had such a passion for flying and often rented a plane on our dates to show me what the world looked like above the clouds.

Everything was lining up perfectly for my career path. I had submitted my application, I did great on the SAT entrance exam, I was accepted, and the scholarship was the icing on the cake. I knew I didn't want to be a burden to my parents. This had to be God's will for me, but in my heart I struggled. This was the opportunity of a lifetime, right? Josh and I had spent a lot of time dreaming about our future together after college, about being married and raising a family. We agreed on almost everything, though he wanted only one or two kids, and I hoped for at least six or seven. We dreamed about where we might live and talked about decorating our future. All our plans were falling into place, yet something didn't feel right.

I cried out to the Lord, "Who am I God? What do you want me to do? Where do you want me to go?"

I was staying with Dan and Patty Distler for a few days over the summer. Dan had been my youth pastor in Cincinnati when Josh and I had met. One afternoon when their family left for the day, I stayed at the house to babysit their youngest child. While the baby was napping, I decided to turn on some music. As I was turning on the stereo, I picked up a cassette tape of a sermon that caught my eye. I read the words: "Relinquishing Your Rights" by Joy Dawson. I wanted to resist—it sounded hard and heavy—but my heart compelled me to listen.

"We have the awesome privilege, tremendous opportunity, and incredible accountability because of free will to say to God, 'You create in Heaven the greatest possible plan for the extension of your Kingdom worldwide through me. I relinquish every right you have given me as a human being. I give them back to you for the greatest possible plan that you can create for the extension of Your Kingdom at any cost to me.'"

"Do you trust me?" I felt Jesus asking me. I trembled. I wasn't sure if I could truly say those words to God. I knew that praying a prayer like that meant surrendering everything. I thought of Jesus who surrendered everything for me, even when His everything included crucifixion. Could I give up everything for Him and His plan to use me to extend the Kingdom of His grace, love, and redemption in the world? There were a few things I was willing to let go of, but I realized that Josh wasn't on that list. I knew if I was going to give myself completely to the purpose of God, I had to surrender everything, even the hope of sharing my future with the one I loved most on this earth.

I listened to the tape twice before I dared to pray. I knew I couldn't say that prayer unless I was willing to live it.

"Lord Jesus, this is my prayer, with or without Josh. I love him, and I want to marry him. We believe that marriage is your

will, but you are bringing me to a place where I care absolutely nothing about pursuing the things of this world. I just want to see You work through me to touch the lives of as many people as possible, that they would spend eternity with You, and yes, this is more important to me than someday becoming Josh's wife. Yes, I surrender. I give up my right to happiness in the world, safety, security, shelter from tribulation, freedom from persecution, and freedom even from hunger. I give up my right to the comforts of this life, my own needs, even my own life, if I can serve you to a greater extent. Jesus you are my joy. You promise to bring me though tribulation. You were also persecuted. You will provide for me and keep me strong, even in famine. I will be clothed in Your righteousness, and if I suffer for Your sake, I will remember Christ who died upon the cross, for me.

"Lord, I am at a place in my life where nothing is hindering me from doing anything you may call me to do. I am free to go where You lead me. Send me Jesus. I am free to do what You want me to do, only empower me Jesus. I want to serve You. So I surrender everything and ask You to prepare for me a plan, the greatest plan You can come up with, no matter what the cost on my part. I surrender my will, my plans, my desires, my rights, my life for Your kingdom. I give myself to You. I am nothing on my own. But I can do all things because You stand by me and strengthen me. I will abide in You and wait on You. Reveal your will to me and to Josh.

"I believe that you have called me to be Josh's wife, but now I hear you calling me to build more than an earthly family. Are you calling Josh, too? I don't want to stop serving you to the fullest when I marry him. Please let us serve You in a greater way as one in You, for Your pleasure, glory, and eternal purpose. And as we build an earthly family, may we build a heavenly family, too. Lord be glorified. In Jesus' name, amen."

TO GO ALONE

I knew it was time to let go of my plans to go to college before I had even said amen. I had no doubt that I was being called to follow the path of the missionary—I was going to the ends of the earth. I would say goodbye to Josh, believing that someday the Lord would bring us back together and we would be married. But for now, he would be the only one going to college, and I would follow a separate calling. It was time to tell my parents.

Josh and I were riding in the back of the white van with my mom and dad when I spoke up. I told my parents that God was calling me to be a missionary, and I wasn't going to college. For a moment, everyone was quiet. I looked out the window at the fields and farms of northern Indiana stretched as far as I could see waiting for their reply. So much had changed since we left Florida just a couple of months earlier.

My mom spoke first: "Ever since your friend Janice went to Hungary to serve the Lord, I had a feeling that would be your lot, too." Then we all talked more about what this decision would mean, and we all had peace. I had no idea how, where, or even when I would be a missionary, but I knew that the Lord would take me there soon. I had a strong feeling that there was a missionary woman praying for someone to come help her with her small children, but how would I find her? As I pondered these things quietly riding along in the van, I had another strong feeling that I should write to the pastor of the church we went to when we lived in California, Pastor Chuck Smith, the same pastor who dedicated me to the Lord when I was a baby in California. A moment after that, Josh turned to me and said, "Maybe you should write to Pastor Chuck." Before I had a chance to tell Josh that I had the same thought, my dad called to us from the front seat, "Hey Sarah, why don't you write Chuck Smith a letter and…" I knew my first step. I needed to write a letter.

With summer over, my family headed back to Florida. I felt like I was letting go of everything I knew in exchange for so many unknowns. One evening, I walked alone on the beach. The sky was dark and clouded in the east, but the sun was shining from the western sky. The charcoal clouds gathered above my head, and before I could make my way home, a gentle rain started to fall. But the sun continued to shine, and a rainbow filled the sky, brilliant and bright above the ocean. My tears mixed with the rain.

I knew I needed to write that letter to Pastor Chuck, but I was afraid. Where would I go? How could I leave? When would I see Josh again? Would Heather be okay without me? Would I be okay without her? We were already drifting apart, and that scared me. Was this calling really from God? How could I know? I looked up at the rainbow as its colors intensified. The rain stopped. What about money? I couldn't support myself, could I? I thought of my tiny income of about $50 a month that I earned from selling my handmade jewelry in a gift shop in a tourist town on the other side of Florida. I couldn't see how anything would work, but I already had taken the first step and informed the college that I wasn't coming that fall.

Even if I knew where I was going, money would be a problem. My parents lived on a shoestring, selling art for a living, and always had just enough. I returned home full of doubts. I was beginning to think that even writing Pastor Chuck was a lame idea, too. He was a pastor of several thousand people, after all. Would he remember me? He did sit by me once in the cafeteria at Youth Camp in California. And he used to tell me that he loved to see my smile when he was preaching because I reminded him of his daughter Cheryl when she was my age. He once said he could see the joy of the Lord in me. But it had been nearly two years since we talked at camp.

I stood in the dining room worrying about money, thinking of the cost of plane tickets, and rehashing in my mind all the reasons why I would be a bad missionary. *I just don't have the faith,* I told God. The phone rang, shaking me out of my dark moment of fear.

"Sarah? This is Mrs. Sullivan from the art gallery in Sanibel Island, where we sell your jewelry?" said the woman on the other end of the line. "I have some bad news. We had a fire; our entire gift shop was destroyed along with our inventory that included all of the jewelry you were selling on commission. It's such a shame, such beautiful work.

"There is some consolation," she continued. I tried to breathe. "Our insurance will be covering everything, and I just wanted you to know that a check will be arriving in the mail shortly for about $1,200—the full value of all of your pieces. We do plan to reopen in a new location, and we are hoping you will be able to restock our inventory and continue to work with us."

I hung up the phone knowing that God was answering my prayer and showing me that He was able to take care of the money. I got out some paper and wrote a letter to Pastor Chuck.

September came, and I had nothing to do but make jewelry out of clay to restock the gift shop, write letters to Josh, take walks on the beach, babysit my niece Elissa, collect shells, and check the mailbox for letters. It had been weeks since I wrote to Pastor Chuck, and there had been no reply.

A month later and still no word from Pastor Chuck, Heather came running into the house with some interesting news about something she found on the beach. I grabbed my camera and went to see what all the excitement was. An empty boat had washed up on the shore. I took photos and began to do some research. What an amazing story that boat told, about a family that fled from the shores of Cuba and was rescued by the Coast Guard. I wrote up all the details and submitted the photos and information to the local newspaper. A day later my photos and story were on the front page.

Suddenly life got even more exciting. My sister Linda was in labor and wanted me to come with her to the hospital. I tried to think of everything she might need for peaceful delivery. I showed up with a CD player, relaxing music, flowers, and massage oil. I didn't know what else to do, so I made it my mission to help her feel as peaceful as possible and make sure the nurses were meeting her needs whenever she had questions or concerns.

As I sat in the hospital room waiting for my new nephew to arrive, the phone rang. The editor of the newspaper where I had submitted my story was calling. Why on earth was he calling me in Linda's delivery room? Apparently my parents had given him the number; he was offering me a job as a newspaper reporter. I took the job on the spot, and not long after hanging up the phone, Linda pushed her baby out. I was one of the first to welcome Rowan to the world while the nurses helped my sister. As I looked into the face of that little boy, I thought of Josh and our future and longed for the days to come when I would bring our babies into the world. That dream seemed so far off, but it was burning in my heart.

So, I began working as a newspaper reporter and enjoyed all my assignments. I began to look forward to the paper delivery in my driveway every morning to see what photos and stories the editors chose. I was amused to see my name alongside the articles almost every day. I also was amazed to be collecting checks every week to add to my bank account. I was beginning to feel like I was wrong about being a missionary and gave up hope that Pastor Chuck would write back. I began to think about making other plans.

One day I went to the mailbox and found a letter addressed to my dad, but he passed it to me.

"Sarah, here is something you might be interested in," he said. I opened the letter to read about the new Calvary Chapel Bible College in Szeged, Hungary. My heart stirred, and at the same time, peace washed over me. As I read about the school, I felt compelled, called, and a little confused. I dialed the number on the pamphlet and asked for an application. About a week later, the information packet from the school arrived at my house. With mixed feelings I began to fill out all the paperwork. Why did I feel so drawn to this place but so uninterested in going to the school? My answer came in the mail a few days later.

I went to my mailbox hoping for a letter from Josh but instead found a letter from Pastor Chuck. I went to the beach to open and read the letter. He wrote about a missionary family in Szeged, Hungary, with three tiny children who were working at the new Calvary Chapel Bible College. He was certain that I would be a blessing to the family and told me that if I would be willing to go help them, he would buy my plane ticket. He suggested I go as soon as possible before the next semester started.

I was going to Szeged, Hungary! A couple of weeks later, another letter arrived from Pastor Chuck; this one included a check for $1000. I was ready to book a flight for the day after Christmas.

An Unusual Job Offer

I never expected to fill a bank account with a newspaper reporter's income or insurance money from a burned-down gift shop. I was sorry for doubting that God would provide for me. I was going to serve Him as a missionary. I was sure of it now, but an unexpected opportunity was about to come my way.

That fall, I had written a news story that caught the attention of a man who was the publisher of a large newspaper in New York and also in England. He was vacationing in New Smyrna Beach, Florida, and was reading the local paper. He contacted me and invited me to visit; he wanted to talk about my work for the newspaper. When I arrived for our meeting at his beach house, half a dozen grandkids greeted me at the door and invited me in. Enormous windows looked out over the ocean. A formal dining room table was topped with beach toys. Children laughed and played.

The elderly gentleman was surprised that I was an 18-year-old homeschooled girl. He was a very old man himself but with a spark of youthfulness in his smile and the wisdom of years in eyes. After the brief moment of surprise, he led me out to the porch where we sipped iced teas. He told me his life story, as the waves rolled in and washed back out to sea. He talked and talked as though the sun would never set. He told me about the old days, about the Great Depression, about washing clothes in the river, and about how he came to own all those newspapers.

Next he wanted to hear my story. It was much shorter. He said that I had unusual talent, and after being in the industry for 50 years, he said he knew talent when he saw it. After two hours of conversation, it was time for me to go. But before saying goodbye, he told me that he would love to have me working as a reporter for his newspapers. He asked me how much I was earning at the small town paper, and he laughed when I told him. He gave me the contact information for one of his Florida newspapers and said that he would let the editor know that he was personally sending me his way. I told him I was getting ready to move to Hungary to be a missionary. He told me he was offering me the opportunity of a lifetime.

I couldn't sleep that night, so I sat up on the roof. The moon came up. The moon went down. Still, I sat. Why did this man come into my life and offer me a dream job just before I was supposed to buy my tickets to Hungary? Should I really go to Hungary? Should I be a newspaper reporter? Did God send this opportunity my way? I loved seeing my name on the front page of the newspaper. I loved investigating stories and photographing interesting things. I loved sharing my opinions and writing my stories. This was the opportunity of a lifetime, right? More choices. Once again I was face with two paths, two opportunities, two dreams, two callings. I found myself asking God the same questions, again. *Who am I? What do you want me to do? Where do you want me to go?*

After much wrestling, I made my choice, contacted a travel agent, and booked my flight to Hungary. On the day after Christmas, I said goodbye to my family, my country, my job with the newspaper, my beach, and my heart. I wouldn't see Josh again for many months.

I knew this was my calling but the details were still a little unclear, even as I was flying across the Atlantic. All I knew was that a guy named John Chebek would be picking up me and a few Bible college students at the airport in Budapest, and then we would take the train to Szeged.

I was quiet as I gazed out the window of the squeaky Hungarian train. I had just left everything I knew, and now I was on a train in a strange land with strange people with little else but a Bible in my hands. I knew that Jesus was with me. When I arrived in Szeged, a light snow was falling. John dropped me off at a cozy bungalow around midnight. An American missionary named Marilyn gave me a pillow and blankets and offered me a cup of tea. Her smile warmed me the most. It was late, so we didn't have time for conversation.

Students from all over the world began to arrive over the next few days. They all spoke English, and they all had a passion for the Bible. Everyone was busy getting the students situated, and I didn't really know how to fit in. Most of the students were new and didn't know how to fit in either. I was sharing a room with three girls: Zoesia from Poland, Estera from Romania, and Gynoyi from Serbia. We were all feeling shy and quiet until Zoesia made tea for everyone. I showed the girls my scrapbook. The ache in my heart for my little sister began to fade as I learned how to build new relationships with other girls, my sisters in Christ.

Before classes started, I met the director of the Bible college, Tim Anderson. He asked, "So, what will you be doing here?" I was surprised that he didn't know. I shyly explained that Pastor Chuck had sent me to help his wife with the kids.

"Oh," he replied. "I didn't know that we needed help with our kids. Maybe you can help Marilyn. She's the librarian."

I was confused. I needed to be alone. I needed to hear from God again. I needed to know why I was here. Was this a mistake? Jesus spoke to my heart, "Do you trust Me?"

Years later, I found out that Pastor Chuck had sent a memo to Tim simply saying that he was sending another person to be on staff. He didn't say who I was or why I was coming. They didn't know that I was being sent to help the Anderson family out with their little children. They joked that maybe I was a spy.

LIBRARIAN FOR A DAY

With a willing heart, I set out to become the librarian's helper. It was a crisp and sunny morning when Marilyn and I took a bus and trolley to a storage room on the other side of the city where all the books were waiting to be sorted. The city was beautiful, even in the bleakness of winter. I quickly fell in love with the colorful buildings and brightly dressed Hungarian grandmas who rushed up and down the sidewalks. Many of the ladies were selling seeds, flowers, berries, or eggs.

Marilyn and I spent the morning in a dimly lit room without windows. We were organizing hundreds of books: theology books, biographies, commentaries, inspirational Christian stories, devotionals, and textbooks. I felt at home there in the stacks. At noon Marilyn said, "Let's go upstairs and take a break. Laura is expecting us for lunch." I didn't know there was an upstairs, and I didn't know who Laura was.

We climbed the stairs and knocked on a door at the end of the dark hallway. Two of the world's cutest little faces popped out to greet us. One of the little girls took my hand, quickly sat me down on the couch, climbed up beside me, and handed me her favorite storybook. She was three. Her name was Claire, and she stole my heart. Meredith, the five year old, joined the story time. Baby Luke played with toys at our feet. Laura Anderson's joyful smile made me feel like I was right where I belonged.

The lunchtime was full of laughter and chatter, and we discovered that little Claire was quite a storyteller. But when the kids finished eating and ran off to play, Laura asked me the same question that her husband Tim had asked me days earlier: "What will you be doing here?"

I was feeling very shy at the moment, but I knew I had to tell the truth.

"Last summer, God put it on my heart to help a missionary family with their kids," I explained. "So I wrote to Pastor Chuck, and he asked me to come here and help you. But if you don't need help, I can . . ."

I looked at Laura, tears running down her cheek. She told me how hard it was for her to move to Hungary and how challenging it was in this city with a baby and two little girls. So last summer, she began to pray that the Lord would send someone to help her. Now she knew that God had heard her prayer. I wiped a tear from my cheek, too. Yes, God had sent me, and I was right where He wanted me.

From that day on, every morning at eight I would join the Bible college students for morning devotions and a time of worship. Then I would walk to the bus stop and head to the Andersons' home, always arriving at exactly nine. I would often pick up a loaf of bread or some pastries along the way. Those little children became the joy of my heart. I would stay with them all day, reading stories, washing dishes, babysitting, watching reruns of I Love Lucy, laughing with Laura, and learning how to be a mommy.

On Tuesdays and Thursdays, I would spend the day alone with the little ones while Laura taught the women's discipleship class at the college. On other days, I would help with the shopping. Sometimes we would all bundle up and go to the park. I helped Meredith with her first reading lessons. I watched baby Luke learn how to walk. I listened to hundreds of Claire's stories about when she was a "little" girl. She was becoming a big girl now, almost four.

I thought I was there to be a blessing to the Anderson family but quickly learned that God had sent me to be blessed, to learn what it is to serve Him. Laura showed me how to be a loving, patient, trusting wife. She helped me to understand that we are all human, with weaknesses, limitations, and quirks, but God loves us all anyway and chooses to let us be part of His plan. I learned that if I fail, I couldn't give up. I have to try again, and rest in the grace of God.

Laura told me as many stories as Claire did, about living a life of faith and watching God provide. I smiled, knowing that I was one answer to her many prayers of faith.

MIRACLE IN A BOTTLE

Josh wrote to me every day. The mail came twice a week, and a few letters accumulated for me on each delivery. There was no email back then, no Skype, and no cell phones. It would have cost $5 per minute to talk on the phone. So we wrote letters, bought airmail stamps, walked to the post office, and waited two or three weeks for the letters to arrive.

My mom and sisters often sent me letters, too. In a letter, I learned that my older sister, Charity, had taken over my bedroom after her rocky marriage came to an end. God was working in her life, and she and Heather were becoming close friends. As their relationship grew, I began to wonder how I fit into our family now. We weren't little girls anymore, and suddenly my sisters seemed to be part of another world, one that I couldn't understand.

I received care packages, too. My mom and sisters always sent me boxes filled with wonderful American items, things I couldn't buy in Hungary, including some of the staples of the American diet: macaroni and cheese, chocolate chips, and peanut butter. I also had trouble finding necessities like contact lens solution. I hadn't even thought to look for it until I was almost out. Suddenly, I was in a bit of trouble. I had forgotten my glasses and depended on my contacts to see. Without them, I could only see clearly for about ten inches, and everything else was a fog.

I wrote to my parents asking for contact lens solution, and the package arrived just in time. But when I tore off the wrapping, I found that they had sent only saline solution, but no lens cleaner. I knew that I had to be able to clean my contacts or I would get an eye infection. If I had an eye infection, I would not be able to wear my contacts. If I could not wear my contacts, I could not see. If I could not see, I could not catch the bus. If I could not catch the bus, I could not be much of a missionary. None of the other students or staff wore contacts. No one could help me, or so I thought. Again, Jesus spoke to my heart: "Do you trust Me?"

I squeezed out one last drop of cleaning solution, took out my contacts for the night, and just as I started to panic, I remembered the words of Jesus. "Do not worry about tomorrow." Another day passed; evening came. I tried to squeeze out one more drop, and two drops came out. The next night two more drops came out. The next night when I shook the bottle, I heard a splashing sound inside. It was half full. I continued to use that same bottle for six more months, and it never ran dry. Every night I went to sleep knowing God's power and resting in His loving care. That little bottle traveled with me to Romania, to Serbia, and back across the ocean.

When I returned home the following summer, I brought that bottle home with me and didn't stop using it until I bought a big bottle of the new 3-in-1 Solution. Even after coming home, my little bottle of lens cleaner remained half full. With a black Sharpie marker, I wrote the words, "With God All Things are Possible," on that bottle and kept it as a constant reminder that God will always meet my needs, answer my prayers, and send miracles when all my own resources run dry.

SERBIA AND THE CEASEFIRE

During my time in Hungary, there wasn't much talk of the war that raged just a few miles south in Yugoslavia. My roommate, Gingie, sometimes shared her grief as she heard news of the bombings, but mostly kept her sadness inside. Her own city in Serbia was under attack, and American planes had dropped the bombs that killed her neighbors and destroyed buildings in her city. She told me her family turned to the black market just to get groceries because trade embargoes made it illegal to import food into the country. She would go home on weekends to bring supplies from Hungary to her parents. Some of the other students at the Bible college happened to be from Croatia, and we all knew they dreaded news of the violent Serbian attacks that ravaged their towns and villages, leaving thousands dead and homeless. Though our countries were all on opposite sides of the conflict, Americans, Serbians, and Croatians all prayed together for peace. We were thankful for the unity we shared in the Lord.

The war escalated into one of Europe's deadliest conflicts since World War II, but everything seemed so peaceful in Szeged where we lived just 40 miles away. One spring day, Gingie was all smiles. The warring parties agreed to a ceasefire, and Yugoslavia was enjoying a moment of peace. From her perspective, this was the perfect time for me to join her on a trip to her beloved hometown. I packed my backpack with extra snacks, just in case we couldn't buy food, and headed to the bus station where we were joined by two other American students. When we arrived at the bus station, Gingie told us that it was easy to spot the buses heading for Serbia because of the huge amount of black market cargo being loaded. I couldn't imagine how they would stuff so many boxes onto the bus and still find room for the crowd of people waiting for seats. I was beginning to feel uneasy about our adventure as the bus left the station. The situation became even scarier when it was time to cross the border into Serbia. I looked out the window as young soldiers with machine guns searched the cars waiting in line in front of us. Some of the soldiers looked far too young to be in uniform. Some had faces full of pride. Others looked as if they were gripped with fear.

When it was time for the bus to be searched, a group of soldiers began opening the cargo doors and shouting things I could not understand. Another solder with a gun that looked too heavy for his small frame boarded the bus, snatching passports from all of the passengers. He looked into my face with wide and questioning eyes, as if he had never seen an American girl, and then he disappeared with a big stack of passports. It seemed like time stood still as the soldiers unloaded all the cargo from the bus and piled it beside the tall, barbed-wire fence. The passengers on the bus fell silent; my friend Gingie assured me that this was normal protocol and everything would be all right.

An hour must have passed before an older man in uniform boarded the bus, shouting orders. All the passengers began to rise from their seats and funnel out of the bus. We were near the back as we watched and prepared to go ourselves. The border guard pushed his way through the aisle with just a few passports in his hand. Suddenly he was standing a few steps from my seat handing back our passports to my friends and me. In broken English he said, "You stay, you are only children." It was just the four of us who were left on the bus as the soldiers shouted orders to the crowd just outside. The bus pulled away as we watched the men and women who had been with us just a few minutes earlier form a line against the fence that divided the two countries, a small wall between war and peace, as kid soldiers held tight to their guns.

We spent only three days in Serbia. The streets of Subotica

were dark and filled with rubble, and emptiness hung in the air. Gingie pointed out buildings that had been bombed and told the stories of heroes and victims. Over the weekend, we visited a zoo full of scrawny animals and bought pumpkin seeds from street vendors—there was no other food. We visited the only market still open and found only a few packages of flour and some eggs for sale. The shelves were bare, and all of the other stores were closed. War had never felt so close, so heartless. This was nothing like the far-off images flickering on CNN; this was real life for real people. Real life and real death.

On Sunday, we walked past abandoned tanks and over piles of scattered rocks on the way to church. We joined a small group of people for worship at the Calvary Chapel in the city, and in the midst of devastation, they sang with all their hearts, clinging to God in ways I couldn't understand.

When the weekend ended, I was eager to return to the peace and safety of our refuge on the other side of the border. How close we were to such horrors, and I hadn't even known. We took a train back into Hungary, hoping to avoid the situation we encountered on our first border crossing. But our return was not uneventful.

When the train stopped just before leaving Serbia, a border guard once again began collecting passports. He seemed angry with us and was speaking words we couldn't understand. He referred to "Americans" in an unfriendly way as he opened our passports, searching for something he obviously couldn't find. Gingie looked fearful this time as she conversed with the angry man. He called her off the train and into the border station. She turned to us and whispered, "The ceasefire has ended, and all Americans must be registered with the police when entering the country. I didn't know! Now you must pray!" So we prayed, and we waited. My parents didn't even know I was in Serbia. Josh didn't know the danger I faced. God was with me, and I knew that my life was in His hands, but I felt so foolish for boarding that bus in the first place. I had no idea what war was! I didn't know that a ceasefire could be so fragile and would end the day after I arrived. Now the war was back in action, and my fellow Americans were flying enemy missions in the sky above. It was a long time before Gingie and the border guard returned to the train. Gingie silently slipped into the seat beside me and didn't say a word, but under her breath, she was singing, "Yes, Jesus Loves Me." The guard held up passports one by one. Some passports were returned to their owners; other people were called off the train like before to line up by the fence. I heard my name called. I worried that I would be left standing by the fence this time.

The man opened my passport and avoided eye contact as he quickly stamped the page and pointed back to my seat. I was free to go, and Gingie's face broke into a smile. A few minutes later, the half-empty train carried us back into the safety of Hungary, and I told myself that in the future, it might be wise to stay out of countries that happen to be at war with the United States. I wrote a letter to Josh on the train ride back into Hungary, but I decided not to tell my mom and dad about my misadventure until a few years later. I didn't want them to worry.

First Kisses

While I was in Hungary, Josh was in Indiana training to be a pilot. But in the fall after I arrived back in Florida, he would be starting college at Embry Riddle Aeronautical University, just a thirty-minute drive from where my family was living on Bethune Beach. I didn't expect to see Josh until he came to Florida for school. The summer dragged on. My parents were traveling a lot with their usual summer art fairs, but they didn't take Heather and me with them as often. They were enjoying their freedom, and so were we. I spent many hours painting, walking on the beach, and baking. Mostly, I was waiting to be with Josh again.

I didn't know what I would be doing with my life until Josh and I were married, but I wanted to be serving God and loving children again. I heard that my favorite musicians, Scott and Christine Dente of "Out of the Grey," had two little children now: a baby and three year old. So I wrote them a letter, told them about the work I had been doing in Hungary, and asked if they needed someone to travel with them on tour to help with the kids. I never really expected to hear from them until my phone rang and Christine was on the other end of the line inviting me to join them for a week later in the summer.

The week on the road went so well that they invited me to join them for three months during the Gravity Tour that fall. I would be leaving Florida just a few days after Josh arrived in late August. It seemed like we would never be together for long until our wedding day. Then, we wouldn't ever have to be apart. A lifetime together sounded wonderful to both of us.

That summer I was turning 19, and Josh told me that he couldn't wait to give me my birthday present. One afternoon, just a few days after my birthday, Heather answered a knock at the door. It was Josh. He had rented an airplane and flew all the way from Indiana to Florida, alone, to visit me for my birthday. He had talked to my parents about his plans in advance, but I had no idea.

I was taking a nap when I felt someone kiss my forehead. Startled, I looked up at him. Was I dreaming? I wasn't sure at first. I stood up, looked around, looked at him. He was all smiles and had a bouquet of flowers behind his back. I hadn't been in Joshua's arms since we said goodbye at Christmas before I flew to Hungary. We held each other for a long, long time. Another moment to cherish our whole lives.

A few weeks later, Josh moved to Florida, and I moved to Nashville, Tennessee, to begin a whole new chapter of my story. I spent weeks watching America pass by from the windows of a tour bus. My life was a string of concert venues, sound checks, coffee breaks, toddler games, hotel rooms, and three restaurant meals a day. We drove all night and woke up in a new city in a new state the next day. We even traveled in Canada for a few days. I spent the mornings with the band members, always in search of a Starbucks. In the afternoons and evenings, I took care of the little ones. It didn't take long for those two children to fill my heart and make me want a dozen kids of my own someday.

I loved everything about being on tour: the traveling, the music, the people, the flights that zigzagged around the nation, and the tour bus that brought me to Maine at the height of its brilliant fall colors. All that was missing was Josh, and how I missed him! He missed me too and couldn't believe that I was traveling with his favorite band. When the tour ended in December, I headed for Indianapolis to spend Christmas with Josh's family.

One evening, we took a walk to the playground in Josh's

neighborhood, the snow falling quietly around us. Our footprints were the only ones in the freshly fallen powder. The world was white and pure. Josh led me to our special place, the place where we had many long and precious conversations over the years. He told me how he had wanted to give me my first kiss there, all the way back on July 4, 1993, when I came from Arkansas for the camping trip. But in that moment he had prayed, and God said no.

Now, we were here again, enjoying the beauty of the snowy December morning, holding hands. I looked into his eyes, the color of the ocean—today they were deep grey. He brushed a snowflake from my cheek, and as the chilly winter wind sang through the leafless trees, Josh dropped to his knees and asked me to be his bride. Then, he kissed me.

We began to plan our wedding for May 1998. I would be 21. There would be Anna Roses and Lily of the Valley. We would be married on the hillside where we camped all those years ago, where we watched the sky and the fire and felt our love come to life.

When we were both back in Florida after the New Year, I began to fill a scrapbook with wedding ideas, and we took many long walks on the beaches, basking in the joy of the coming days. A thousand prayers were being answered. A thousand hopes fulfilled. The promises of God unfolding. Only two more years.

The thought of waiting that long after experiencing the passion of his kisses was like torture. We didn't want to enter into the relationship of marriage until we were ready to start a family. We would have been married sooner; I was ready at age seventeen. But we knew that Josh needed to finish college first. His plan was to devote himself to completing four years of school in just two and a half. By taking 21 credit hours of classes each summer, he would meet his goal to finish school before the summer of 1998.

We treasured the sweet days of our engagement. In the beginning we simply enjoyed the new freedom from some of the limits we had placed on ourselves. We quickly realized, though, that we needed to find our new line before we went too far. We couldn't handle the feelings that came with the pleasure of losing ourselves in each other's kisses. We were committed to saving our deepest passion for marriage, so we came to God and asked for wisdom to know where to draw the line. We realized that it belonged right where it was before we were engaged. The kisses and the unquenchable passion that came with them would have to wait until our wedding day.

So we waited.

The Phone Call

It was one of those phone calls that you never want to get.

My parents had moved to Oregon, and I was living on my own in Florida, two hours south of where Josh was going to school. My mom called to give me the news that my grandpa in Arkansas was dying of cancer. I felt so helpless and so far away. I wanted to visit him but had no money. My mom had a better idea. My grandpa needed a nurse to live at the house to help care for him: would I be willing to move to Arkansas for a few months, take some nursing classes at the hospital, and move in with my grandparents? If I was willing, my grandpa would be able to leave the hospital and live in his own home. I said yes.

No one expected my grandpa to live much longer, but I was determined to give him the best care I could. I had studied nutrition, so I knew that juicing raw fruits and veggies could help. I also introduced my grandparents to trace minerals. On the first day home from the hospital, my grandfather had a severe reaction to one of his medications. I quickly did some research and found out that two of his medications were incompatible and taking them both could even be fatal for someone in my grandpa's condition. I contacted the doctor right away and asked him about the prescriptions. Sure enough, one of the doctors had made a mistake.

My grandpa had good days and bad days, but over time he grew stronger. I saw him laugh again, joke again, and get out of bed again. I stayed with my grandparents until my aunt was ready to move in next door and take care of them for the rest of their days. I was so thankful that I was free to share my life with my grandparents in that difficult time in their life. How sweet it was to see the love of a husband and wife who had shared more than 50 years!

I had a lot of freedom between the end of high school and the beginning of marriage. I had asked God to make me someone's angel. I asked him to show me where He needed a pair of gentle hands, a loving voice, a listening ear, two feet willing to walk an extra mile, a friend for lonely orphans, a cook for a crowd of hungry travelers, a helper for busy moms, a nurse for my sick grandfather. I knew I wasn't skilled. I knew I wasn't educated. But I was willing to try anything. I was willing to learn. I was willing to give. And mostly, I was willing to love.

Serving

I look back on those years feeling so blessed to have had all those wonderful experiences of serving God. When I was helping people, I knew that I was doing the work of God, growing in faith, seeing miracles, and making the most wonderful friends. The hardest part of my calling to be someone's angel was that I was constantly being called away from my sweet lover, my patient, faithful, precious love. But Joshua knew that I was serving Jesus. Every time we said goodbye, he would just hug me close until the last call was made for boarding the plane. We longed for the day when God's calling on my life matched God's calling for his life and we wouldn't have to be apart. But in times like these, Josh gave me freedom, and I was free to be an angel to help others in times of need.

All through life, both Josh and my parents have been so trusting, so supportive, so encouraging to me in my calling, knowing that I was in God's hands. Instead of telling me what to do or trying to keep me close, they encouraged me to trust in God, to love God's word, to rely on the Holy Spirit, and to walk by faith not by sight. If they ever feared for my safety or security while I was in Russia, Romania, Hungary, or even in Serbia during a war, they never showed it. The ones who loved me most gave me to God, and gave me their love—and prayed a lot.

Years later, the day actually came when it was my mom and dad following God's calling into one of the most dangerous places in the world: South Sudan. My sisters and I were shocked when they casually announced that they were going to Sudan to be missionaries and work in a place where people were shot by rebels all the time. They were going to a place where children were kidnapped and forced to kill, where people died for lack of medical care, where most families had very little to eat, and they themselves would be living on beans and rice and an occasional butchered goat.

Suddenly I was the one having to trust my parents into the hands of God. I really worried that they might not come back. I worried that my kids may have to grow up knowing that their grandparents were kidnapped by enemies or shot to death in Africa. But if I was worried, I didn't tell them. I just prayed, put my faith in God, and sent them off with a blessing. It was my turn to trust them into the hands of the Lord, and God has been gracious to us all.

How did I know how to trust them into God's hands? My parents taught me.

WINDOWS OVER AUSTRIA

While I was counting down the days until our wedding, I was learning to follow God and be brave, to let go of Josh for a time and set out on my own again. It was much harder to say goodbye now that we both were living in Florida and were seeing each other every weekend, but I still had a desire to serve God overseas. Particularly, I had a burden for Russia, and when the opportunity came, I knew I needed to go.

I had heard that things often get mixed up when you make plans to travel to Russia. My experience was no exception. It was June 1ˢᵗ, and I was reviewing my travel documents as I packed up and prepared to leave. I held an airline ticket in one hand, my travel visa in the other. My ticket to Russia said, "June 4, 1997," but my visa said I could not enter Russia until July 1, 1997. I had a flight to catch in three days, but I wouldn't be allowed into Russia without that visa. I spent the day on the phone with embassies, airlines, and everyone I knew in Europe. The airlines explained that I had to fly out of the United States on June 4ᵗʰ, or I couldn't fly at all. The lady from the airlines also said I could take a one month «lay-over» in Holland, and then continue my flight to Russia in July.

I saw my plans fall apart, but my mom said, «Maybe this is God's way of getting you to a destination you hadn't expected. Maybe the Lord has better plans.»

Three days later Josh took me to the airport again. He held me for as long as possible, whispering prayers and precious words of love. I was wearing an engagement ring this time, and when he let me go, tears rolled down my cheeks. My arms ached with longing to hold on to him just a little longer. I wanted nothing more than to be his bride, but it wasn't time yet. We had to say goodbye. This may have been the hardest goodbye. We were no longer children. This time it was a man and a woman ready to be husband and wife who parted in the airport that day.

The flight across the ocean was like a dream. Though I had planned to go to Russia, instead I found myself waking up the next morning in a castle in the Austrian Alps. The castle had been transformed into a conference center for missionaries. What could be more rejuvenating than sunlight and roses, wild strawberries and mountain air? Somehow I ended up with two perfect jobs for the month. In the mornings I would serve breakfast to the castle guests. Then I would spend a few hours on the hillside designing and planting rock gardens in the afternoons. How quiet, how beautiful, such perfect peace. From the hillside, I could look over the lake that filled the valley below. I was surrounded by mountains, green with forests and dotted with pastures of grazing sheep.

Most afternoons I would follow a trail into the village of Millstatt in the valley. My first stop was always the post office to collect the letters from my future husband who wrote nearly every day. I followed the winding cobblestone streets past the ice cream shops and bakeries of the seven-hundred-year-old village to find the perfect spot to read my precious letters. As I looked out over the lake and hiked through the emerald mountains, I hoped that someday I would walk these paths with Josh. So I filled his mailbox, too, with letters expressing the painful longing of my heart. I was ready to be completely his, to share his home, to wake up in his arms every morning, to meet his needs, to wash his socks, to kiss him with no more boundaries, to have babies together, to raise a family, and to follow one calling instead of two.

On my way back to the castle, I would follow the lane that ran along the lake. There was a dock and a few small boats that I was free to use in the afternoons. I would sometimes hear singing down on the dock below the castle, as the valley echoed with the voices of Christians from all over the globe singing to God. How could I not be moved to worship Him too? I was surrounded by the glory of His magnificent creation. Why had He brought me to this beautiful place? I was on my way to a dirty Russian city. I was ready and willing to work hard, endure sacrifice, give up all my comforts, and even suffer for His sake. But why was I suddenly living like a princess? I sat on the dock, and wondered about all the blessings, peace, and beauty that surrounded me. This wasn't the life of a missionary that I had expected!

One afternoon as I looked out the windows of the prayer tower, I realized that perhaps God wanted to show me what it meant to be a daughter of the King, His own dear child. When I was a young girl, I had pretended to be the lost princess of the forest, living like a pioneer in the woods behind my house. Now, here I was walking through the halls of a real castle. I think God wanted to show me His greatness, His majesty, and His Glory. He wanted to spend hours walking with me on mountain trails and listening to my prayers and songs from this tower. He set aside these days of my life to show me His love. He wanted to get me alone one last time before I became a wife and mother. This was *our* season, and it was His joy to lead me to a castle, beside the still waters, tucked in the mountains of Austria. It was His delight to restore my soul, and it was His pleasure to remind me that I truly am a daughter of the King, and the Bride of Christ.

My mom was right. I was exactly where God wanted me. Though my plans fell apart and life seemed all mixed up for a while, God was on the move.

In Russia

"So what are you doing here in Russia?" one of the missionaries asked.

"I'm teaching some children's ministry training classes for anyone who wants to learn how to teach Sunday school," I replied.

"So you enjoy working with kids?" she asked.

"It's my passion. There is nothing more I would rather be doing," I told her.

"We have a team coming in from Florida, and we want to put on a Vacation Bible School for street kids. Can you help us with it?" she asked.

"Sure, what can I do?" I asked. I was willing to do whatever I could.

"Well, most of all we need someone to organize everything and plan all the games, crafts and activities . . . and tell all the volunteers what to do." She smiled.

I froze. I never saw myself as a leader. I thought she was going to give me a stack of yellow paper to cut out some butterflies. Or maybe I would pass out the snacks or help the kids decorate T-shirts. But she was looking for a leader.

"Sure, I'd love to!" I said. Even as I heard myself saying these words, I didn't mean to say yes. But some kind of courage had come over me. "When does the VBS start? How many days do we need to plan for?"

I pulled out a notebook and started taking notes.

"Okay, how many volunteers do you have? Do you know how many kids are going to come? Maybe 50 or 100? Okay, so we need to be flexible. Is there someone who can lead the songs? What about translators—I'm guessing that your team from Florida can't speak Russian?" My mind raced, and I got to work, still not sure what I had agreed to.

That night I was on my face before God. "I'm not a leader. I can't do this. Remember me? I'm timid and quiet. I'm not good at planning things. I'm not good at organizing things. What am I going to do with 25 volunteers? I can't speak Russian." I whined, I doubted, I feared. I opened my Bible.

"Don't be afraid. I promised to be with you," I heard Jesus say in my heart. "I will give you wisdom, strength, and ability to do everything that I call you to do. Trust in Me. Rely on Me. Depend on Me. I can handle this, and I will show you exactly what to do. I created you to be a leader, just follow Me."

The children poured in from the streets, dusty and dressed in rags. There were more than could be counted, but we had enough love to go around. We offered music, and every child learned to sing "Jesus Loves Me" in his own language. The tables were set up with games, crafts, and coloring projects. We told them all about Jesus. I was mystified when the volunteers came to me for instructions, advice, and guidance. They were looking to me to lead, so I pushed aside my feelings of inadequacy and led them. As I looked out over the busy volunteers and all the joyful children buzzing around and working on projects, I realized that I was made for this.

One evening, I took the underground metro train to a neighborhood where I had never been—St. Petersburg is a big city. I was going to be teaching a class on children's ministry that night, and a friend went with me to show me the way. We had such a fun night, though I was amazed that I had to teach adults how to be creative. Creativity was a new concept to these young Russian adults who just a few years earlier had lived under Communism. We made puppets out of paper bags and people out of pipe cleaners. We were like kids again. When we finally looked up at the clock, it was almost 11. No one knew how late it was because the sun never sets in St. Petersburg during the summer. The friend I came with rushed out the door to get back to her family. I cleaned up the supplies and packed my bag, and then I headed out the door, too.

I thought I knew my way back to the metro station, but after about ten minutes of walking in the wrong direction, I realized that I was lost. Instead, I tried to find my way back to the place I had just come from, but I looked around to see that I was surrounded by dozens of identical Soviet-style apartments. Now I was *really* lost.

Earlier, I had walked along a canal and near a big lake between the metro and church where the workshop was. I also knew that we had been very near Main Street. I was convinced that if I could get to one of those three landmarks I would be able to find my way back to the Metro Station. So I picked a direction and started walking. But I never came to the lake or the canal or Main Street. Soon, it was midnight, and I was still walking the desolate streets, alone in a sea of concrete buildings.

I had no cell phone—no one did—and there were no people around or businesses open. All I could do was ask God to help me. I bowed my head, closed my eyes, and prayed that God would help me find my way. Peace came over me. I lifted my head, opened my eyes, and looked around. I was standing in front of the steps to our church; above the door was the familiar sign with a picture of a dove and the words "Calvary Chapel" written in Russian. Of all the places in the entire city, this was the one place I knew my way home from. I was certain that the last time I had looked around apartments surrounded me, but after I prayed, I found myself on the doorstep of my church. I stood trembling at the answer to my prayer.

I was lost, but He found me. I could not find my way, but He helped me. Once again I knew that I could trust in God. My life was in His hands, and he had promised to be with me. I had a new song in my heart as I walked to my Russian home underneath the midnight sun.

"I DO"

When I arrived home from Russia that fall, I moved back in with my parents in Florida, seeing Josh every weekend or so. Josh worked hard to complete college ahead of schedule as planned; he even graduated with honors, magna cum lauda. We were counting down the weeks until our wedding, making plans for the big day ahead.

For seven years I had known that I wanted to be Joshua's bride. Seven years seemed like forever, but May 16, 1998, finally came.

Our families gathered on the grassy hillside as a few cottonball clouds floated above. A white horse and carriage brought my father and me to the edge of the forest where my future husband waited. He hadn't seen me in my wedding dress until that moment. Two or three hundred people turned to see me walk down the grassy aisle, but of course I didn't see any of them. Just as I had planned, I carried roses and lilies, surrounded by ivy and lace.

This was the day, the hour, the moment. He was the one I had waited for, and I was his virgin bride in a white dress. I would be his, and he would be mine for the rest of our lives, come what may.

As husband and wife, we joined hands, kissed, and held each other tightly. For years, we had shared one dream and one hope. Now, we would share one life, beginning a family of our own. We would live together in one home. We wouldn't have to say goodbye at the end of the day. We wouldn't have to resist each other's passion. We were free to wave goodbye to our friends, our siblings, and our parents, and build our own life together. The waiting was over, and we belonged together. No more letters.

The horse and carriage waited for us at the other end of the aisle. My husband and I climbed in and disappeared down the lane. We wanted to spend our first twenty minutes of marriage together—everything else could wait. We had waited for years for this moment, and now it was ours. We looked at each other and our wedding rings, and he held me close. In those few minutes alone, I listened as he prayed for our new marriage, our future, our life together, placing everything in God's hands. He asked the Lord to show him how to be a husband, how to love me, treasure me, serve me, care for me, and provide for me all the days of our lives. I knew I was treasured; I knew I was precious. I was everything that a bride could ever wish to be because I was so deeply loved.

I knew that the love my husband had for me was more than just affection or friendship, more even than passion and desire. Our love for each other and our life together began in the heart of God. We were created for each other. We knew that God had entrusted us to one another to live one life together We knew that the wedding was just a beginning, and we would share many other firsts and new beginnings over the years. It would be a life full of purpose, beauty, harmony, purity, kindness, forgiveness, sacrifice, compassion, and peace. It would be a life of faith. We would make mistakes. We would have trials. There would be hurts and hardships. But all these things would bind us closer and make us stronger. Together we would discover our calling, touch the world, give life to our children, and maybe create a spark to light up the lives of others.

But for that moment, we just held each other close, thankful and joyful, knowing what it feels like to belong.

As the sun set on our wedding day we were thankful for our seven years of waiting, hoping and preparing for our journey to begin. A long winding road soon led us to a peaceful log cabin deep in the wooded hills of Brown County, Indiana. Now we belonged to each other, we both knew we were safe in each other's love and free in each other's arms. We were building a marriage that would last a lifetime, one built on the rock of faithfulness and faith, a life full of hope. From the very first day, being married seemed so right. Even though our future wasn't clear, our present moments were pure joy. We didn't know where our adventure would lead us, but we were willing to go anywhere, as long as we were together following the footsteps of our Maker.

Within a few days of saying «I do,» we left Indiana behind, bid farewell to our families, and crossed an ocean for the first time together. I wanted my husband to come with me to Austria, to look out of the windows in the castle at Millstatt, to explore the villages and ride the European trains to places we never dreamed we would go: Germany, France, Italy, Spain, Bohemia, and even to Hungary.

Spring turned to summer as we camped along the peaceful Danube River. The mountain peaks rose high, and the villages were sweet. We never knew what a day would bring, but one of the greatest joys was to wake up in my husband's arms each new morning. We were lost in Venice for hours. We borrowed a pair of bicycles to explore the Spanish coast. We played in the Mediterranean sea. We bought a pregnancy test in Budapest, Hungary. We walked for miles through vineyards and orchards, with seven years of history and a lifetime ahead to share.

We didn't bring much with us - backpacks, a camera, a map, a tent, our Bibles and a pair of European rail passes. One evening as we camped, I sat by the fire, watching as the light flickered on the pages of the Bible in my husband's hands. He flipped to 1 Corinthians 13 and read out loud the secrets to a life of love revealed in that chapter. We knew life would never be the same.

MAR
TIRRENO

Just for Tonight

Just for tonight let me hold you
Just for tonight let me lay my head on your chest
And listen to the rhythm of your heart
I don't want to fall asleep too soon
So I can treasure these hours
Feeling your arms around me

Let's open up the windows and listen to the music of the night
Let it be the only sound,
Beside our thoughts, our hopes, our memories
Come be with me

Just for tonight I feel like being quiet
Just for tonight I could talk the whole night through
All I know is that I've longed to be with you
Come be with me

Remember how we longed for each other
Counting the days, the hours, the minutes
And then the moment would be ours
And nothing else mattered just to be with you
Come be with me

Let's open up the windows and listen to the music of the night
Because nights like this are the nights we used to dream of
Nothing else to do, but to know that I'm with you
Come be with me

Set aside all the things all these things that crowd our lives
And make time for the one thing that matters most
Nothing else to do, but to be holding you
Come be with me

My heart's delight in that I am now yours and you are mine.
The years, the hours, the minutes bring us to this promised time.
And I will hold you, like there is nothing else in the whole world to do
Come and hold me too

And I will be with you

Come be with me

PART 3

GIVING LIFE

A New Little Person
Comes Along

I looked out the window of the airplane on our way home from our honeymoon. I was amazed, not by the ocean below, but by what was happening within me. We had been married only two months! We had thought about waiting a couple of years before starting a family. Now, a new life was growing inside of me, and in nine months, a new little person would arrive just in time for our first wedding anniversary. Surprise!

Josh could not contain his joy. Everyone on our flight back to America knew that he was going to be a daddy. We were having a baby. We would be parents. He wanted everyone to know. He loved putting his hands on my tummy, while whispering prayers and promises.

I was very curious about the progress my tiny child was making in my womb. So I got a copy of As Your Baby Grows. The book showed photos of unborn babies at every stage. It was unbelievable; my little boy was starting to take on the shape of a baby at just three weeks. I didn't know that unborn babies looked like little people when they were just a few weeks old!

As the weeks continued, I often whipped out a fetal development book to show people photos of my unborn baby's current stage. I'd say, «Can you believe that at just five weeks the baby already has fingers?» Or I'd tell people that at seven weeks the tiny person has toes, is sensitive to touch, and already wiggles around. If there were a window to the womb, I might have caught my 16-week-old, unborn baby sucking his thumb, doing flips, and playing with his umbilical cord. I even knew a woman who said if she had known that the 20-week-old, unborn baby was more than a blob of tissue, she would not have had an abortion. She felt lied to by the people in the family planning office where she had turned for help when her boyfriend left her alone. Her story broke my heart.

When I reached my fifth month of pregnancy, the baby began kicking really hard whenever the music at church would stop. After he was born, he was so quiet during the singing, but between songs he would cry as if to say, «Sing some more!» I knew before Isaac was born that he loved music!

When my son came into the world, I was overwhelmed with joy as I held him in my arms for the first time. Each time my husband spoke to him, Isaac lifted his chin and turned his head to look into his daddy's eyes. He knew his father's voice already. We were parents; this was our child. He would be coming home with us. We thought that we knew what love was, but our little son had come to teach us that love is something stronger, deeper, richer, fuller, and more powerful than anything we understood before. It wasn't just the love of a parent and child that amazed us, but the depth of love we experienced in our marriage as we began a new chapter together as mommy and daddy.

FARM GIRL

Living on a farm was always a far-off dream until I had an excuse to make those dreams come true.

In late 1999, fears of Y2K began circulating. When clocks rolled past midnight to the year 2000, many feared the modern world and all its technology would crash as computers tried to process a new century. Josh and I were newlyweds living on the beach in Florida when Aunt Joan came to visit. We were quite content with our lives; I was a stay-at-home mom, and Josh was a flight instructor at Embry Riddle University. Josh also had started a small computer repair business called Need-A-Nerd? Computer Service. I would sometimes paint the windows of shops for the holidays in my free time. We had everything we needed, and life was comfortable.

«Y2K is coming!» Aunt Joan had told us during her stay. In her anxiety, she insisted we needed to learn how to survive without technology because life as we knew it was coming to an end. Sounded like fun to me, so I did a little research on pioneer living and considered putting a chicken coop on the balcony of our beach house. But then Hurricane Floyd came, and we decided that a chicken coop on the balcony wouldn't be such a good idea. Besides that, the neighbors and local zoning laws might have had something to say about chickens, too.

About the same time, my friend Shaunna gave me a pile of *Country Living* magazines depicting country life in the Midwest. I had visions of a white cottage in the country, homegrown tomatoes, clucking hens, fruit trees, and fresh herbs in my window boxes. I dreamed of seasons and porch swings and the state fair. I wanted to raise a big family out where the corn pops up in rows, where the green grass grows tall and thick. Josh was excited about the idea of going back to Indiana to be involved in his home church again, Horizon Christian Fellowship, the church where he met God and where we were married.

When Hurricane Floyd's two big brothers came, we had to evacuate our Florida home, and as it turned out, we evacuated all the way to Indianapolis for a few days. During our visit, we took a drive out in the country, and before we returned to Florida, we were convinced that Indiana would be our home. Job opportunities were available for my pilot husband, and he knew he could rely on his talents in fixing computers to support the family in the meantime. So one month later, we closed the sale on our own little white house in Fortville, Indiana, and moved in just one week before Christmas. My farm girl dreams were starting to come true on the three beautiful acres in Indiana.

ANNA'S HOMEBIRTH

Y2K came and went, and the world didn't end. Winter passed, and spring floated in on the scent of cherry blossoms. We marveled at the colors of tulips from our front porch swing as we waited for our second child to be born. Our family of three was about to become a family of four.

On a Tuesday morning in May, I brought in a big bouquet of peony flowers from our garden. I had been waiting for them to bloom—I wanted to fill the house with bouquets of them to make the house welcoming for the new baby who was expected any day.

Later that afternoon, Josh's friend Jay called to see if we had the baby yet. He asked if I wanted him to pray that it would come now. I told him it was our second anniversary and we were going out that evening. He said he would pray that the baby would come after dinner.

That evening, I ate more than ever—a big steak, salad, potatoes, and more. Then, Josh and took a walk around downtown Indianapolis. The city lights were bright, but the nearly full moon was even brighter. I wanted ice cream, so we went to Steak 'N Shake. As I ate my strawberry shortcake sundae, we talked about Isaac's 14-month-old words for things. We were laughing about how he calls the moon a "boof" when I felt the first real contraction. Six minutes later, I felt another. It was almost 10:00 pm., so we went straight home and called the midwives. We were planning a homebirth.

Josh and I picked lots of flowers by moonlight between contractions. My mom arrived and helped Josh prepare the house, while I relaxed in the shower. The midwives arrived around 11:30, and we all sat around in the living room while

Josh played guitar and sang to me. Mom rubbed my back during the contractions. Sometimes I would make Josh stop playing and rub my back, too. Sometimes I would sing with him. Josh's mom arrived to help with little Isaac. At around 2:00 am, everyone but me took naps. I took a long bath by candle light and quietly sang praise songs to help me ease away the pain. The contractions grew stronger and longer, but I was able to relax and let my body do its job. Being at home was so peaceful.

I didn't let Josh sleep long. He comforted me and massaged my back as things got more intense. I kneeled at the end of our bed for a while on my hands and knees. I had nice long breaks in between contractions, or the pain would have been unbearable. Mom and one of the midwives took turns rubbing my back, helping me breathe slowly, and encouraging me. I decided to take another shower, and to my surprise the sun was rising. Morning light streamed through the windows. I had no idea that the whole night had passed.

When I got out of the shower, I was feeling a lot of pressure and wanted the baby to come out, but I didn't have the strength or urge yet to push. So I went out and sat on the porch swing. One of the midwives, Sandy, brought me some juice, and a plate of pears and cheese slices. In spite of the difficult contractions and the pain coursing through my legs, I was still having nice long breaks in between, sometimes 4 or 5 minutes. I began to relax again.

When they came, the contractions rolled in like powerful ocean waves. Sometimes I would close my eyes and just keep breathing, and sometimes I would stare out at the morning mist over the trees and fields. Sandy spoke to me of that new baby smell, of tiny baby toes, of a warm baby at my breast. My mom was praying for me. I was able to find greater peace, greater than the pain. Still, I dreaded the feeling of another contraction taking over. Sandy reminded me that I would have only as many contractions as I needed, and each one brought the baby closer to being in my arms.

Soon, I began responding to the contractions a little differently, and Sandy asked me if I was still planning on having the baby in the bedroom or if I would like to give birth right there on the porch. I opted for the bedroom and headed back in. The midwives put the finishing touches on the room, lighting candles and bringing in vases of peonies.

I knew the baby would be here soon, and a desire to bear down increased. Josh sat behind me in a chair as he supported me; I was squatting. The midwives called in my mom and Josh's mom with little Isaac. With the first real push, my water broke, and the baby's head crowned. With the next push, the head emerged, and with the third push, the baby came «flying out," as Josh later described it. Little Isaac watched it all, quiet and interested.

I took our baby in my arms and put her to my breast right away, holding the beautiful little one close.

«Well, what do you have?» everyone asked.

"A girl," I said. "A little girl."

Our daughter gazed at her daddy, so alert, so sweet, like she knew his voice.

We welcomed her into our arms, into our family, and into our home. We prayed for her, thanking the Lord for her. We named her Anna.

Sarah's Journal

Purity and Peace

I am passionate for purity and peace. To quiet my heart and set my spirit free. Purity and peace, I follow after these. That's what I love about the ocean. I can walk along the shore and look out to the horizon and for as far as I can see God's creation is before me.

I love the shadows of the forest, below the summer leaves. I love to find a grassy clearing surrounded by the trees. I love to look into the sky, and as far as I can see, beyond the clouds and blue so deep, God's creation circles me. I can feel sweet purity and peace.

I love the winding paths, carved in the mountainside. I love the rocky trail, and my husband by my side. I love the peace and purity we share, if we are lost in the valley or looking into the starry sky from the highest places of the earth. I feel so free just to be in a place where there is nothing more to see but God's creation, sweeter yet when my lover shares the view with me.

We have hiked to mountain tops. We have touched the star-filled sky. We have watched the silver moon rise above the silver peaks. He holds me close and kisses me as the stars circle the sky, delighting in the treasured gift of purity and peace.

I have kissed the sweetest lips and walked in moonlit waters. I have splashed in clear blue streams with all my little daughters. I've followed squirrels with my son. I've joined him in the trees. I've laughed so hard I couldn't speak.

I've made a chain of daisies. I've worn a flowered crown. I've waited hours with a child, a shooting star to see. I'm happy, and I'm free, with family all around. Peace comes with their smiles, and treasured purity.

Eggs in my Pocket

Anna was just a few months old when Josh looked into her baby face and said to me, "She's not a newborn anymore, let's have another one!" He was only joking, but a couple weeks later I told him the news! Anna and Issac were soon followed by a little sister, Estera, who arrived just as the tomatoes in the garden were ripe enough to add to the salad. It was August of 2001.

Though I was a mommy to three children under three years old, I wasn't too busy to start living my farm girl dreams. Isaac was now big enough to be my helper, and we thought it would be fun to have a few pets. It was time to build a chicken coop, some fences, and a small barn.

While I was cooking, cleaning, planting veggies, and tending babies, Josh was devoted to establishing a computer business in Indiana. He had to let go of his flying dreams after struggling with health problems that caused migraine headaches. We were both sad to find out that he didn't qualify for a medical certificate in flying anymore, but we trusted in the Lord who blessed us. The computer business quickly grew, and it also gave Josh the freedom to make his own schedule. He needed to work only four days a week to meet the needs of the family, so he had spare time to help me build a barn and some fences. I didn't grow up in the country, of course, and I hadn't spent more than three minutes with a goat or chicken until the day we drove home together in the minivan with three pregnant goats in the back. I smiled at my sweet husband—he would never have imagined the adventures waiting for us when he married me.

I learned one of life's great lessons on that little farm: do not put raw eggs in your coat pocket. I was new at this "farm girl" thing, but I quickly realized that it was a bad idea as soon as I dropped the fifth egg in and heard that dreaded cracking sound. My husband's yellow rain coat was a mess, and I had two less eggs for the carton. That day I also learned not to leave the lid off the goat feed, especially when rain clouds are on the horizon. Then I learned to shut the barnyard gate just a little faster. Before I even knew what had happened, I was pulling a stubborn goat out of a garbage can full of wet feed with cracked eggs in my pocket.

But I loved being a farm girl. I loved being a mommy. I loved chasing goats in the rain and tasting the sweetness of sun-ripened strawberries and wild tomatoes. I loved Hurricane Floyd for driving us out of Florida. And I loved Aunt Joan for telling us that Y2K was coming, even though it never did.

First Year of Homeschooling

As the children neared school age, Josh and I knew that we would homeschool them. After our first year, we couldn't have been happier with our decision.

In those first few months, I watched Isaac unlock the mystery of reading. With his new-found power, he set out to happily (if not slowly) read anything that sparked his interest. I also taught him the basics of math and then watched as he put all his learning together and started a successful jewelry-making business, not unlike my own childhood venture.

Apart from the basics, Isaac also took a special interest in fossils, so we took trips to Ohio and Florida to learn more. Our greatest surprise came when he found and identified a trilobite in a friend's rocky driveway. Isaac also was fascinated with maps and started a globe collection, often looking for them at garage sales and thrift stores. He had fun comparing the changes that history made on his globes. China became one of his favorite countries, and he got excited every time he discovered a "Made in China" sticker. He also learned some of the sad stories behind those stickers, like the deplorable working conditions and child labor in factories. The missionaries who gave their lives to reach China with the Gospel became his new heroes. He wanted to learn Chinese, and he happily ate fried rice and noodles every chance he got.

Isaac also became a little builder, dreaming up projects with leftover wood from the mini barn. Anna followed him everywhere, and wanted to be his helper. Sometimes we took special trips to Home Depot so he could learn about all the different types of nails, latches, and power tools. One day he taught his little sister how to hammer nails correctly, and no one got hurt.

LIFE IN THE YELLOW HOUSE

In the Summer of 2002, we sold our little homestead and moved into a huge yellow Victorian House on Main Street in Fortville. A few months later, our fourth child, Rachel, was born and quickly adapted to the pace and rhythm of family life.

In our new home, we were two blocks from the historic downtown but still only two blocks from the nearest farms. Our home was unlike most others I'm sure. One room was filled with musical instruments. Our sunroom served as a library, although there were piles of books in every room. We had no TV, and instead, we had a craft and game room. We used board games to teach math and had hours of fun with paint, clay, beads, glue, and paper. I had as much fun as the kids when it came to education. I'm so happy that our home became such a rich place for learning, discovery, and creativity.

We moved to Main Street to have more space for all the new friends who were becoming part of our lives. In 2001, we had started a community garden and Trading Post for moms and kids. It started with about five families from church, but within months, 50 families were involved! Our old house was too small to host every one. When I saw a "For Sale" sign go up on Main Street, we knew what to do. Our little farm house sold quickly, and we moved our goats and sheep to the Apple Family Farm a couple of miles away. We missed the farm life, but we loved being part of a close-knit community in our charming Midwestern town.

The concept of trading with others was something that made sense to me. Why use money if you have something else of value to exchange? As a young mom without much extra money, I thought of all the fun I had had as a child trading with the artists during those summer art fairs with my family. So, twice a month on Saturdays, 30 or 40 local women and countless children would fill my home with all the things that they wanted to trade. My tables would be stacked with fresh baked breads, homemade jams, fresh brown eggs, plants, herbs, yarn, spices, soaps, craft supplies, and anything that grows in a garden or on trees. I created a point system so we could trade fairly, every point being worth twenty-five cents. There were always a variety of things to choose from, and we would all go home with baskets of pleasant things we would have never had time to produce alone or spare money to buy.

As we traded all our homemade and homegrown products, we began to exchange other things too, like parenting tips, talents, recipes, babysitting, homeschooling ideas, and our favorite books. The Trading Post soon added a library and a classroom where women could take turns teaching skills, and before long, community began to take shape. This was not a community of houses and neighbors, but a kinship of families who loved home-centered living. We renamed ourselves the Simpler Times Family Co-op.

My family later joined a professional trading company. My husband fixed computers for the businesses in the network and was paid in "barter bucks" that funded a car, a vacation, a washer and dryer, a new floor, trees, haircuts, landscaping services, and gift certificates for many local restaurants.
Learning to trade, share, give, and make things of value at home was an important part of my life, beginning all the way back with that little blue box I traded for my mom's small painting, and a little bit of courage. I've learned not to let a lack of money get in the way of living a life rich in good things and interesting people who are willing to make a little swap, or maybe a big one.

ISAAC AND THE DIMES

Isaac was five years old when he was given a toy that changed *my* world. I can't remember who gave the gift, and I don't think a thank you card was ever sent.

The toy was a Lego robot space man warrior who arrived in about 50 pieces in a plastic box that said, "Ages 7+." Isaac was very excited about it and dumped out all the pieces, studying the wordless building manual intently. I thought for sure Daddy would end up putting all the pieces together, but I didn't say anything. At least it would keep Isaac busy for a while. About an hour later, a very proud little boy was showing off the robot man he built. And Daddy didn't help him at all. I had all the mixed-up feelings of a mommy whose baby was growing up too fast. Then, I began to wonder what else my little man might be capable of. A few days later when all of the Lego man's pieces were lost, Isaac asked if we could go to the store and buy another one. I asked him if he had eight dollars. He checked his pockets and said, "No, do you?"

"Isaac eight dollars is a lot of money," I told him, "and you have already lost all the pieces of your other Lego man. If you want another, you will need to earn the money yourself."

"Sure mom, I can do anything. I just need a job!" he said, smiling. So I made a little chart.

"Think of eight jobs that you can help mommy with," I explained. "You can earn a dime for every time you help. After you do each job ten times we will go to the toy store."

He thought for a few moments and announced confidently, "I can make all the beds every morning. I can set and clear the table when we eat. I can load the dishwasher. I can sweep the floor. I can clean my room. I can put the laundry in the washer and dryer. I can vacuum. And I can babysit the girls (his three little sisters)."

He got started working before I finished making the chart, and once again I had all the mixed up feelings of a mommy whose baby was growing up too fast.

Isaac spent the next two weeks proving that he was very capable of accomplishing every task he set his heart on. With pride, he would lead me to his chart on the refrigerator so I could draw a little dime in the box after each job was completed. Soon, my little girls joined in on the adventure. Anna mastered the art of sink washing, and Estera spent her playtime hanging up the shirts and dresses. Rachel picked up the Cheerios she had dropped on the floor.

I found myself feeling more and more like a queen and less like the mother of four helpless preschoolers. I spent my time reading books, eating grapes, cuddling the baby, and designing royal crowns with my little girls. It was a happy day for the whole family when Isaac had earned all 80 dimes. We all took that trip to the toy store together. Isaac had accomplished great things, and we were all so proud.

As we stood in line waiting for the cashier to count all of Isaac's dimes, a woman spoke up with one of the comments I had started to hear over and over again. "Oh! My goodness! Are they ALL yours? You must have your hands full! How do you do it all?"

"I don't," I replied, smiling. Then I told her the story of Isaac and his 80 dimes.

Old-Fashioned American Dream

I grew up in the 1980s believing in the old American Dream.

The dream that put a 20-pound turkey on the Thanksgiving table.

The dream that included a pretty young mom, in a red, white, and blue apron and a smiling daddy with a baby on his knee.

The dream included about a half-dozen kids asking for more pumpkin pie, with grandparents, aunts and uncles nearby.

Most of all the dream was all about finding the love of my life, winning his heart and falling in love. Marrying young and raising a house full of kids sounded wonderful to me.

It was a dream about a family sharing life, my family, watching the fireworks on Independence Day, having picnics, playing baseball, building snowmen. It was a dream that included the love of my life with me on a porch swing growing old together. In my view, life wasn't about a career; it was about the making of a family. It was a dream inspired by Norman Rockwell's paintings on the cover of the Saturday Evening Post.

The idea of having my own home and being the mommy was almost magical to me. When I was fourteen I had my life all planned out. I wanted to have seven beautiful daughters, who would spin around in beautiful dresses singing of "rain drops on roses." They would be like princesses or characters from a Jane Austin novel. I would have a huge Victorian House filled with treasures from all over the world. My life would be full of adventure.

I would have an adventurous husband who would show me the world, make enough money to support my dreams, and have lots of free time to spend with me. If he couldn't make enough money, I would be a famous artist, inventor, or writer. Call my dream childish. Call me naive. But that was my dream, and I lived my life like dreams come true.

LEARNING AT HOME

When Anna turned five, she joined Isaac with homeschooling. I realized quickly she struggled with pencil and paper. She didn't like workbooks. She just wanted to play, draw, and learn about plants and animals. She was a child who loved to learn from experience. So that year we took many trips to the Children's Museum, Indianapolis Zoo, and the White River Gardens. We also turned our house into a tiny zoo complete with fish, frogs, and kittens.

Our garden proved to be one of the best classrooms of all. We turned the garden into a big science project, and all of the children claimed areas of the garden for their own. It kept them all busy.

Isaac happily shoveled compost, laid mulch, lugged rocks, dug holes, and welcomed his payment of a dollar an hour. He put the professionals to shame with his hardworking spirit. When he finished his own work, he helped me collect all the empty flowerpots and began filling them up with soil and compost. He spent the money he earned from his gardening work on flower seeds, planting them in the pots with hopes of a plant sale later that summer.

Anna loved to water everything: the flowers, the trees, even the cars, cats, and her little sisters. She also loved to make mud. Her section of the garden was obvious—she was growing mud pies. Anna also was our budding artist, and mud offered her a fun way to practice her skills. I had to watch her closely, though, because one day I caught her and the little sisters stripped to their undies and covered with mud from head to toe. All you could see of the girls were shiny white teeth and smiling eyes. It was Anna's idea of course. They were "painting."

Four-year-old Estera was the busiest gardener of all. She took over the rock garden around the lamppost and beside the front sidewalk. Every time something pink, purple, or fragrant exited the minivan, she was right there digging a spot in her garden. Often I would find her chewing on a mouthful of chives as she worked. She planted *hundreds* of seeds, and she tended them all with care. Unfortunately, I discovered that she planted half a bag of popcorn kernels in my salad garden, and they actually grew.

Rachel was my little laundry maker. Learning to do laundry was an important educational experience too, and the children learned this skill early. Rachel liked it more than the others, though. The moment she found a speck of dirt or a damp spot on her dress, she was unloading the dryer for me and dumping out her drawers looking for a change of clothes. But only a pink dress would do—she refused to wear anything else. If her pink dresses were all dirty, I learned to stick her in a swimsuit until the laundry finished. She would help me put all the clothes into the washer. Then, Isaac turned the knobs and pushed the buttons.

The garden was a wonderful classroom, but the kitchen was even better. We found that learning fractions from a recipe book was a lot more fun than learning fractions from a textbook. And we discovered the principle of cause and effect when a box of baking powder was secretly dumped into the biscuit dough. It was challenging to get around our kitchen with four little people standing on chairs so they could see better, but turning the kitchen into a learning center was worth the trouble.

Desks, chalkboards, textbooks, and number two pencils just didn't come to mind when my children thought about school. When they woke up each morning, they couldn't wait to start the new adventure of learning. We didn't even have time to get out of our pajamas before the school day began.

Living a Poem

Today, I have wiped lipstick off the faces of my little girls.
I have mopped the floor with old towels.
I have written a love letter.
I have sat in the hammock with three of the children.
I have eaten frozen orange juice on a stick
and cleaned sunscreen from the floor.
I have found lost shoes, and I have poured the milk.
I have watched the birds, the moon, and the clouds.
I saw a hot air balloon rise above the rooftops.
I have ignored the handprints on the windows.
Today, I swept up orange peels, cat food, and raisins from the floor.
I have collected a few lost spoons from the backyard.
Today, I have hung wet towels on the porch rail.
I have kicked a watermelon rind under a bush.
Today I have lived a poem.

IS OUR FAMILY
GROWING TOO FAST?

With four children under five years old, my life was full and busy. There never seemed to be enough hours in the day. There was more laundry, more dishes, and more demands on my time than I could handle. I still loved being a mom, but I was having trouble learning how to do it all.

When Rachel was six months old, I had become concerned about getting pregnant again soon. People were telling me that I would wear out my body and wouldn't be able to take care of the four children I already had. Honestly, I just didn't feel ready. I was back in shape after the last pregnancy and enjoying my slim phase and my size six jeans. I needed some time to get the family prioritized and the housework done.

One evening when all the kids were asleep, Josh and I talked about our plans for our family's future. We both knew that raising a family was a precious calling and a privilege from God. A big family is also a big sacrifice. We wanted to have more children, but was the timing right? Could my body handle another so soon?

"Sarah, we believe that God has a perfect plan for our family," Josh said. I nodded. "We have trusted Him with everything so far. He knows what we can handle, and He loves us. So let's just pray and ask Him to show us in the Bible if He wants us to prevent having another child right now."

So before we opened the Bible, we prayed together, believing that God would answer this very important question. My husband put his arms around me and held me close to his heart, running his fingers through my hair and loving me sweetly. I was at peace. When he reached for his Bible, I knew that our answer would come from the God of Love—*He* treasured me even more than this husband of mine did.

We were in the habit of reading the Bible together every night, like we had done since we were young teens. Always before the goodnight kisses, Josh prayed with me and read at least one chapter. This evening we happened to be in Luke 18. "Then parents also brought infants to Jesus that He might touch them, but when the disciples saw it, they rebuked them. But Jesus called to them and said, 'Let the little children come to Me and do not forbid them, for of such is the kingdom of God.'"

I smiled at Josh, he smiled at me, and we both said, "I think we have our answer!"

So we let the little children come. But to our surprise, I didn't get pregnant for another six months. I believe God knew that I needed rest, and when the timing was perfect, we conceived again. When the news came that another baby was on the way, I felt ready. I was rested, strong and at peace.

Isaac and Anna were happily helping around the house. My parents had even move to Indiana to be close to the grandkids. Josh's business was well established, and he had more free time than ever before to spend time with the kids and me. We were also enjoying a higher income as well, and a trip to Italy was in our plans! My parents could see that Josh and I needed a break and offered to help with the kids so we could get away before the new baby came along. We were blessed and knew that all these wonderful blessings came from God.

LOST IN ITALY

We heard the sound of the approaching train as we waited at the small Italian station. I was a little unsteady, more than six months pregnant with our fifth baby. It was 2005; Josh and I were in our late twenties. This trip to Italy was our last chance to use our free tickets to travel, just the two of us, before the baby came. As the train slowed to a stop, an announcement was made over the speaker. We didn't understand Italian, but we should have gotten a clue when half the waiting crowd relocated to another platform. We got on the train anyway.

We ended up traveling for hours in the opposite direction of our destination, but we had that familiar feeling that we were in for an adventure. Over hills and rivers, past towns, through tunnels, and out of Tuscany, the train whizzed through several stations, rarely stopping and barely even slowing down. We soon realized we were on the fast train to Rome. We studied our maps and guidebooks and made new plans. There was a walled village in the hills that could only be navigated by foot after crossing a narrow pedestrian bridge over a ravine. It sounded fun and romantic, so my husband agreed to attempt a new destination. When the train finally came to a stop in an unknown city, we hopped off. Josh carried all the bags.

My husband had a way of communicating with the Italians that always seemed to enrich our experience. He mixed broken Spanish with the few Italian words he knew, throwing in some English and a lot of laughter and animation for good measure. From his conversation with a man at a bus station, he determined the way to the walled village. So, we boarded a bus with dozens of school children, some of whom spoke a little English. We showed them the map; they laughed at us.

We were relieved to be moving in the general direction we hoped to go until suddenly the bus changed directions. That familiar feeling of adventure ran through us again. In a bus instead of a train this time, we traveled again over hills and rivers, past towns, through forests and farmland. The bus made frequent stops until all of the school children were dropped off. Once again, we studied our maps and guidebooks, but this time we were clueless. I was starting to worry. The sun had begun to set, and the wind carried with it the chill of autumn. Storm clouds gathered in the west. We were lost in a beautiful place, but the idea of a late night walk across a rickety, narrow bridge over a steep ravine was sounding a little less romantic, especially at six months pregnant. At least my hero was still by my side.

The bus stopped. The driver turned, surprised to see us still there. He shooed us off in broken English: «No more bus. Stay here; tomorrow new bus. Walk to city.» Just like that, the bus disappeared down the street. Josh laughed. I cried. Then I started laughing, too. We made our way down the tree-lined cobblestone street. When we came around the bend, we lifted our eyes to an ancient castle that rose above the trees into the purple sky. Just then rain began to fall, even though the sun was still shining. A far-off crash of thunder sent us running hand in hand to the shelter of the castle. We were royally wet as we climbed the great stone steps and passed through the iron gates. In amazement, we stared around the courtyard. It no longer mattered that we were lost. It didn't matter that we were wet. It didn't matter that we didn't know where we would stay the night. We found shelter together in a castle.

The rain slowed to a drizzle as we climbed the spiral staircase to the turret high above. We were speechless as we looked out to the view below. The setting sun cast its rays over the water of a great lake to our west. The lake was surrounded with villages, towns, and fortresses, all with the warm glow of light in the windows. We felt as if we had been whisked into another world, another time. A stone village surrounded the castle, and we watched as an old man navigated the narrow, cobblestone walkways on his bicycle. The streets were like a maze winding through the quiet village. A barking dog broke the silence. The glow of the village grew brighter as the sun sank lower, casting a deep golden light. Then the rain stopped, and we watched the village come alive. People moved about, and church bells rang out from the east.

"Sarah!" Josh's voice was full of awe, "come with me, but don't look at the sky until I say." He took my hand and led me to the northern catwalk of the castle. We were running now.

"Okay look!" he shouted. The cross on a church's steeple rose into the eastern sky, all aglow under the arch of a brilliant rainbow.

That very morning we had prayed a simple prayer, asking the Lord to be with us and lead us and bless us. And He had. I leaned into my husband's arms as we looked to the rainbow and the cross, realizing that God had directed our adventure all along the way just to bring us to this beautiful place.

As we looked out over the beauty of this magical land, our hearts were telling us to gather up the family and move to Italy. An impossible dream? Maybe.

But we had seen impossible dreams come true before.

NAOMI

We didn't need the toy store. We didn't need a TV or video games. We didn't need to go anywhere for fun or entertainment. We had a baby in the house. We had Naomi.

When Naomi was born, Isaac was only six, and she already had three big sisters. I wondered how I was going to manage so many little children. Not only did I get a new baby, but I also got a house full of little mommies, and Isaac had transformed from a carefree kindergartner into his baby sister's hero.

Little Naomi captured our hearts and made our home a place of wonder. When she smiled her first smile, four little faces smiled back. When she got her first tooth, a house full of little people were by her side with teething toys, comfort, and joy. One little cry and she was surrounded by love. One little giggle and our home was filled with laughter. The older girls rarely played with dolls when they had a real baby in the house. The whole family found such indescribable delight when she was born.

I never knew that the milestones of a *fifth* child could be so exciting! Josh and I weren't the only ones cheering Naomi's first steps; Anna and Isaac actually taught her to walk when she was just ten months old. Two-year-old Rachel taught Naomi how to sing, and Isaac started teaching her life lessons about the great big world. Four-year-old Anna always made sure that her baby face was wiped and her diaper dry, and Estera wanted to be sure that all Naomi's clothes were fresh and clean. As soon as the children woke up at the crack of dawn each morning, they would get busy entertaining Naomi, and I would get to sleep in a little longer. It's so nice to have a baby in the house.

For weeks, Rachel kept a running commentary on everything Naomi did. «Mommy, Naomi's awake. Mommy, Naomi wants a snack. Mommy, Naomi wants you to hold her. Mommy, Naomi has boogers. Mommy, Naomi got the cat. Mommy, Naomi's getting the potty. Mommy, Naomi wants to play dress-up.»

Baby Naomi was born right after Christmas, and all the other gifts were forgotten.

Like all the other children, I knew that Naomi would grow up fast. Babies are babies for just a little moment in time. But for those first few weeks after Naomi was born, I couldn't imagine life without a baby in the house.

An Orphan's Hope

Before Naomi had even taken her first step, I sat bouncing her on my knee on the steps of a Jamaican orphanage, looking out over the valley where the rest of the children were playing. I couldn't be happier—Josh and I were finally serving God together at an orphanage with our own children. A young boy name Jermain sat with me, and he poured his heart out to me.

Jermain spoke about his mother, whom he hadn't seen in years. He told me he also never saw his brothers and sisters anymore because they all lived in different homes. He just wanted to be part of a family. As Jermain and I talked, we could hear the sound of my husband's guitar echo through the valley. A little group of orphans had gathered around Josh and were singing with all their hearts. My son Isaac had joined Jermain and me for a game of pick up sticks.

"Jermain, what do you want to do when you grow up?" I asked.

He thought for a few minutes and confidently said, "I want to be like your husband, Josh. I want to travel for Jesus and sing songs all over the world, songs about Jesus."

I looked out to where Josh was still playing. "Do you think that you want to be a daddy someday too?" I asked.

"Oh yes! I want lots of boys and some girls," he exclaimed. Jermain was beaming. His little mind had taken hold of a new hope.

"Someday, I'm going to be the kind of daddy that I always wished I had," he announced, determined. "I will have a family. I'm going to take good care of my boys and girls and teach them everything. We'll play a lot of games, and I'll find a good job and make good money. I'll take my family to church every Sunday!"

I didn't know what else to say, so I just smiled at him. Then, Jermain got really serious. "And I'm going to treat my wife the way I always wished my daddy would have treated my mamma," he said. And I knew he meant it.

As he spoke of his dreams, he was clutching a photo of my family I had showed him. He quietly asked, "Can I keep this?"

I wrote a Bible verse on the back of it for him—Jeremiah 29:10-11—then handed the photo back. Yes. He could keep it. He thanked me as he held the picture to his heart. Then he ran off to join the other orphans who were singing along with Josh.

Little Jermain sang with all his heart.

TURNING THIRTY

The weirdest thing about turning thirty was the thought that in ten more years I would be forty. Isaac would be seventeen. *Who knows, I could have ten or twelve kids by then,* I thought. I wondered if we would still be living in Fortville, Indiana. I wondered if the town would change for the better. Maybe we would be living on a farm or be missionaries in a foreign country. Maybe all of the above would happen, or maybe the end of the world would have come and gone. I wondered. Only God knew.

The past ten years had been an amazing journey, and I was excited about what the future held. But before I could look ahead, I thought about each of the past birthdays I had celebrated during that span.

I remembered ten years earlier celebrating my 20th birthday with a visit to Indianapolis to spend time with my fiancé and his family. I spent the next birthday as a missionary in Russia. On my 22nd birthday, I was on my way home from a honeymoon in Europe, pregnant and nauseous and so happy to be married. On my 23rd birthday, I was a mommy of a little boy, and we were living on the beach in Florida. For my 24th birthday, I was a mommy again of a baby girl, living out in the country near Fortville, Indiana. My 25th birthday was also my due-date for baby number three, though she was a week late. On my 26th birthday, we had just moved into our yellow house on Main Street in Fortville, and I was losing my cake and ice-cream, nauseous again for *some* reason. Up until that day, I had never seen a negative pregnancy test, and once again we had good news: little Rachel was on the way.

Life had felt hard the summer I turned 27. Josh was running his own computer business, and I was the mother of four preschoolers. We were raising baby chicks in our back yard—about 500 of them—and I also was doing *a lot* of laundry and dishes. Life was full, and mommy needed a little rest. So we got our priorities straight and got rid of the chickens.

People often thought that two children were plenty, three were okay, and no one has more than four. With four children ages five and under, people often gave me free advice about how to stop the babies from coming. They were the same type of people who years ago couldn't see why Josh and I were waiting for marriage to become physically intimate with each other. We didn't want babies back then, but we welcomed the babies now that we were trying to get settled as a family. I was starting to believe, though, that maybe the dream of having a big family was more than we could handle.

For my 28th birthday, we loaded up our minivan with our four little children and drove to Pennsylvania, Ohio, and Washington, DC. I was just getting over morning sickness, and we had lots of fun showing our kids around the country. The kids were five, four, two, and one, and everything in life was an adventure waiting to be discovered. It was fun seeing the world through the eyes of little children once again. We stayed for a week with a family of ten, and then we stopped in Ohio to visit friends who had 12 children. I noticed how beautiful both mothers were, even after bringing so many children into the world. A few months later, Naomi was born, and I had to wonder if God had sent me an angel. Baby Naomi brought peace and calm into our home and delighted us all with her little smiles.

My 29th birthday was just a vague memory, but my 29th year was the most fun up to that point, thanks to my friend Leslie who appeared in my life right after Naomi's birth. She loved children as much as I did, and since she didn't have any of her own yet, she enjoyed spending time with our family and "borrowing" my children. I always had a house full of kids (mine and all the neighbors). I had a husband who was more in love with me than ever. My back was healed that year after ten years of pain when an old grandmother I didn't even know prayed for me on a Sunday afternoon. Feeling strong and healthy, I was able to do lots of gardening that year, too. I also got back into writing and had a chance to put my life into words for the local newspaper every week.

I also learned more and more about mothering, teaching, and preparing meals for a small army. I had lots of practice with my five small kids, and couldn't wait to try out all the new skills on baby number six who was due the month after my birthday.

Josh and I spent my 30th birthday weekend on Wisconsin's beautiful northern peninsula. He had planned to surprise me with thirty gifts over the weekend, but I think he gave me about a hundred. Our five children spent the weekend with some friends who have seven children of their own, and they all survived. When we returned from Wisconsin, we heard the wonderful news that Leslie had just welcomed her first son into the world. The doctors once said that she may never have children, but God had better plans. As I held her little baby William, my heart stirred with joy knowing that my next child would soon be born, too. We would be mommies together.

Looking back at the previous ten years during that birthday weekend, I found myself simply thankful. Every year of that decade was blessed with joy, and many of the years had been blessed with a *bundle* of joy. When I turned twenty, I thought a lot about my hopes, goals, and dreams for the next ten years. Turning thirty had seemed so far away. But thirty came fast, and I was thankful to have landed right where I was.

When Children Make Mistakes

I'm learning to show my older children grace when they make mistakes. It is very natural to look at the older child's mistake, forgetfulness, immaturity, and failure with a response that says to the child, «How can you be so stupid? How can you be so childish? Failure is NOT an option! I can't believe you did this again! What's wrong with you?» But I must ask myself—how do I want to be treated when I mess up? What did it feel like to be a child shamed in the sight of my parents?

Today, when I fail, what do I desire from the ones who love me? Mercy? Yes. Forgiveness? Yes. Restoration? Yes. Kindness? Yes. Help? Yes. Grace is what I long for when I fail. God our Father responds to his children with mercy. Shouldn't I treat my children the way I would want to be treated? Shouldn't I ask myself, What is the heart of God for this child who has fallen down, who has messed up, who has defied me? It's hard to treat a child with grace when they fail. But if it is grace I want when I fail, shouldn't I give that same grace to others when they fail me? It's easy to judge, condemn, and ridicule. Do I want judgement, condemnation, and ridicule? No, not me—I hope for mercy.

My children are certain to make a lot of mistakes along their paths in life. They will do things that I think are stupid. They will hurt me with their words, actions, and carelessness. They will ignore my plans, hopes, dreams, and desires for them as they follow their own passions, callings, and desires. What will my response be then? I only hope and pray that I will show them mercy, forgiveness, and grace. I need to give them freedom to grow up, to become adults, to make their own choices, to learn their own lessons, and to find their own way.

I hope and pray they will know that there is hope, grace, restoration, and mercy to meet them in the dark, in the pain, and in the rebellion. I don't want to reject them when they disappoint me. I need to hold them and teach them mercy and then guide them into the truth. I want to be like Jesus who said to the woman caught even in adultery, «I don't condemn you; go and sin no more.» If Jesus can have this heart for such a woman, can't I have a heart of mercy for my child who disappoints me with her actions or words? It's hard to love with God's merciful love, but now that I know the grace of God myself, how could I withhold this grace from my own precious children?

May the Lord help me to balance justice with grace as I raise all these beautiful little humans that He has so graciously entrusted to me. May I learn to love them with the compassionate heart of the heavenly Father, who remembers that we are just dust. May I show them mercy starting now while they are still young.

SAILING MISTAKES

Josh and I kissed our kids goodbye, said thank you to our friends and the grandparents who would be babysitting, and hopped on a plane. Our plan was to spend eight days camping in the US Virgin Islands. I was about five months pregnant with baby number six, and we both were ready for a relaxing time in the Islands.

Though Josh had dreamed of going to the beautiful beaches of the Island of St. John, we couldn't afford the hotels there, and all the campgrounds were booked. I found out about a camp in the rainforest on St. Croix that sounded like heaven to me. And it was, even with the night-crowing roosters.

We spent the first four days exploring the Island, learning to drive on the wrong side of the road, and trying out the local food. I would not eat the bull hoof stew, but Josh did. We quickly learned that we were on an island ruled by wild chickens, and I discovered that in St. Croix people don't build fences to keep their animals in—they only build fences if they want to keep their neighbor's free-range animals out. Wild chickens hung around the restaurants with outdoor dining, cleaning up under the tables when the patrons left. When we took a nature hike, we came across a friendly horse grazing in the rain forest. Herds of goats were led to the roadside each day to chomp on weeds. I loved it.

The campground was peaceful until night fell, and I heard some strange sounds outside our cabin. One night, there was a loud chomping, stomping, snorting sound. I woke up my sleeping husband, "There's a critter outside. Can you please go scare it away? I can't sleep." Josh unwillingly rolled out of bed and went to the window. I heard him chuckle. "It's just a couple of big cows grazing," he said, still laughing. As it turned out, the camp gate was left open, and since the neighbors free range their cows at night, we got a couple of visitors.

With all of the animal life, there was never a dull moment. After only a couple of days, I was ready to go back home but only to pack up the kids and move to Wild Chicken Island. We always talked about raising the kids in far-off corners of the world. We wanted them to see that there is more to the world than they could ever imagine.

By day five, I was worn out and ready to relax and put "adventuring" on hold. After all I had just turned thirty; it was time to stop and smell the roses. Josh still had all kinds of ideas about sailing, snorkeling, and finding a way to St. John so we could explore that island too. All I wanted was a cup of coffee. As we sat in Paradise Cafe, I explained to my sweet husband that I really just needed to sit on the side of the mountain, take walks on the nearby beach, watch the sky, read a book, and eat papaya for the rest of the vacation. He put away his Island Adventure magazine because he loved me more than snorkeling.

At that moment, however, a sailor with a wild look in his eye plopped down a pamphlet on the table in front of us. Jason owned a sailboat that he used to take people out for romantic evenings on the calm and dreamy seas. We couldn't get out of the cafe before he was offering us a deal on an evening of sailing into the sunset. I saw a twinkle in my husband's eyes. The sailor made it all sound so lovely, romantic, and relaxing. I took a deep breath and nodded, Josh grabbed Jason's business card, and we said we might give him a call.

A couple of hours later we were packing up all of our luggage and boarding the sailboat for the adventure of a lifetime. Why sail into the sunset when you can sail to St. John for just a few dollars more? We would sail all night, and then, we would spend the next day sailing around the island, exploring coves and cays. At sunset we would sail back to St Croix. A cabin below deck was equipped for sleeping. Jason gave us a great deal, and off we sailed into the sunset.

As my husband helped raise the sails, I looked out over the gentle waters—the colors of sunset filled the sky. We began to drift away from land. All was quiet except for the wind in the sails and the lapping of the waves. The Captain broke the silence with warnings about seasickness and falling overboard. He went on to tell stories of sea storms and pirates. I was glad when he got busy with the boat again and stopped talking.

As the full moon rose over the water, I cuddled up to my husband and looked out over the silvery sea. The island we left behind faded in the distance. The sky and ocean seemed so vast; I felt so small. My mind drifted to the generations that had come before me, who bravely crossed this mighty ocean. The past, present, and future collided in my heart as the boat rose and fell with each wave.

All was well with my soul until the seasickness came over me. Before long, I needed to lie down in my cabin and try to sleep away the nausea. So I curled up in the company of the captain's cat, and all was peaceful once again. Until the storm hit. Rain was pouring in my windows, and the little boat was tossed about, like a child's toy. Josh was on deck trying to help secure the boat, but the storm came up too quickly. They didn't have time to get the sails down. The captain was worried the strong winds would badly damage the boat. My husband didn't have time to comfort me. He simply told me that things look bad and I had better pray.

But I was too scared to pray. I worried that we would disappear into the sea. I worried about my orphaned children. I worried about what I would do with the boat if the men got washed overboard and the rain kept pouring in. Josh came down into the tiny room just long enough to close my tiny window to keep out the rain.

Then I remembered the story of Jesus on the Sea of Galilee.

He was asleep on a pillow, and a great storm came. He slept right through it until his disciples woke him up to tell him that they were all going to die. Jesus got up and said to the wind and waves, "Peace be still." The wind and the waves obeyed his voice, and all was calm. But our storm raged on.

Then, the winds changed, the storm shifted, and suddenly the sea was calm again. All was well with my soul, but I was wet and still a little seasick. The storm had driven us quickly to our destination, and by two in the morning, we dropped the anchor at St. John. The rain continued to fall throughout the morning, and we sat soaking wet, eating oatmeal on the deck. I wanted off the boat.

When the clouds cleared, we hopped into the little dinghy and rode to shore. We found a place for coffee, but I was too dizzy to enjoy it. I told Josh that I wasn't getting back on the boat—I simply couldn't do it. We would have to find some other way back to St. Croix. So we spent the day enjoying the most beautiful beaches on earth, hitchhiking from one location to the next, then camped for the night on Cinnamon Bay. St. John is known as the Island of Wild Donkeys, and I did enjoy it.

When morning came, we had to quickly catch a ferry to another island, where we would catch a second ferry to St. Croix—sailing was still out of the question. When we missed that second boat—it left an hour earlier than scheduled—we stood gazing out to sea wondering what to do next. A seaplane landed on the water nearby, and another adventure came to mind—this time it was my idea. Fifteen minutes later we were boarding that little seaplane, and we were back to St. Croix in time for lunch.

We spent our last days on the island sitting on the side of the mountain, taking walks, building sand castles, watching the sky, reading books, and eating papaya—adventure-free.

Caption: Sail-plan of the Spray.

Keeping the Love Alive

Thinking of my life so far, Josh and I have shared a lot of adventures since we met in 1991. We follow our hearts, follow our dreams, follow our rabbit trails, and try our best to live what we believe. It's been fun. A lot of work too, but mostly fun.

Things don't always turn out like we hope, but one path leads to the next, and what a beautiful and fascinating journey it's been. We have collected so many treasures along the way: friends, memories and lessons learned. I am so thankful that through it all, our love for each other grows deeper and our faith in God is refined. Every dream is tested by reality as we learn to hold on or let go. I feel so blessed to have a husband who isn't afraid to walk by faith. He put's his heart into his passions, works hard, and knows how to have fun. I'm so happy to have a God who is so much bigger than us, who always picks us up off the floor, like a dad teaching His toddler to walk.

Josh and I have been married more than 14 years, and every day is sweeter than the one before. Love grows deeper, and joy keeps stirring. Some people think that marriage gets old and stale as the years go by, but that doesn't have to happen. My mom and dad have been a great example of keeping love alive. Josh and I have seen many of our friends end up with broken marriages, and it is so sad.

Josh has a silly quote he often recites: «Change your life—not your wife!» I guess we are not the kind of people who need the stability of sameness to be at peace! To keep the excitement and fun in marriage, we have our adventures, we do something new together, we take risks while we still have the energy and time to bounce back if things don't work out.

Sometimes, we learn a new skill together, like sailing. Other times, we test our dreams, like moving to the country and then back to town. Sometimes, we get in over our heads on some crazy dream and hold tight to God and each other.

We are learning to support each other's goals, give each other time for refreshment, and save up so we can travel to new places. We see life as a mission we are on together. But even when we can't travel, we can read books together or get a babysitter for a date night. We know we need to say, "I'm sorry," a lot. When life feels out of sink, we ask God for new direction, perspective and vision.

There are lots of things to do together to keep the fun in marriage. The main idea is to be on the same team. Some people say they get dizzy watching our lives. They can't understand why we are always doing new things. We are young, in love, and energetic. We have lots of ideas and dreams. And though our ventures may not always be a big success—sometimes our plans flop—if our marriage comes out stronger, our friendship sweeter, our family closer, and our souls a little wiser and humbler, it was worth the risk.

New Year's Rezzolootins'

"Mommy? What's a New Year's Rezzolootin'?" our now seven-year-old Isaac asked on the last day of 2006.

"A New Year's Resolution?" I replied. "Well, today is New Years Eve, and tomorrow is the beginning of the year 2007. A lot of people like to think about the new year and make a list of what they want to do over the next 12 months."

"Like go to Chuck E. Cheese?" he asked.

"Well, most people make a list of goals or changes they want for the new year," I explained. "Some people want to stop being fat. Some people want to save money for something special. Some people want to change the way they act and be more loving to their little sisters. Some people want to get more serious about obeying God. Some people will decide to read the whole Bible in a year or start eating their vegetables more often."

"Ok, can we get a paper and make my list? I really need to make some New Years Evolutions," he said enthusiastically. "Should I have ten or twenty or a hundred?"

"Well, let's just start writing and see how many you have."

"Okay, Mommy, I'll tell *you* what to write. This isn't school," he said. My smart, cunning boy.

So, he dictated while I scribbled down his to-do list for 2007. We labeled it, "Isaac Brown's New Year's Resolutions."

1. Go to Chuck E. Cheese.
2. Train my cat.
3. Build a Lego city. I mean a BIG city.
4. Learn about airplanes. I know that daddy knows a lot about airplanes.
5. Go Shopping.
6. See Saturn with my telescope.
7. Oh, I do want to go to Florida.
8. And I always do want to learn the violin. But how much would that cost? Seven hundred dollars?
9. I want to get a bunch of chapter books to read.

"What about things you want to change or do better?" I mentioned. So, he added a few more.

10. Ok, have a happy heart when I'm cleaning.
11. Oh yeah, I want to make my own garden. I already cleared a spot behind the barn. I think there's enough sunshine there.
12. I want Granddad to teach me how to build more stuff with hammers and nails.
13. Build a tree house.
14. I want my own little drum set.
15. Keep my room clean.
16. Take a bath two or three times a week.
17. Get some brothers.
18. Read the Bible more.
19. Beat Daddy at Chess.
20. Oh, and I do want to see a Planet!

As I helped Isaac put the finishing touches on his list, I had a feeling that he might just keep most of his New Year's Resolutions. Besides taking a bath two or three times a week and keeping his room clean, the whole list seemed quite possible. And fun.

Learning Traps

I like to set «learning traps» for my kids. Here is how it goes... I open a science experiment book and leave the supplies beside it in the kitchen... and walk away. I get out the sewing machine and put a pile of fabric beside it, plug it in... and walk away. I put a recipe on the counter with a few ingredients and a big bowl... and walk away. I place a monopoly game on the table, open the box... and walk away. I get out a flower pot and set a bag of dirt and some seeds beside it... and walk away. I take three books about cats off the shelf, open them to interesting pages... and walk away. I discovered this method by being too busy to finish my own projects, and soon learned that one of the kids will come along and be inspired to pick up where I left off!

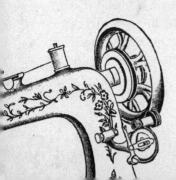

READY TO POP!

"You look about ready to pop! When are you due?" a stranger asked me one day in the checkout aisle of the supermarket near our home in Fortville.

"Oh, last Saturday," I said, smiling.

Her eyes got big, her mouth dropped open, and she didn't know quite what to say. I could tell she was afraid that my water would break any second and the baby would drop out, right in front of her.

"Don't worry," I replied. "My last three were over a week late."

"Uhhh, how many more do you have?" she asked, her eyes still big.

"This will be number six."

"So . . . and then are you done?" she asked.

I smiled. "On no, we are just getting started!" I joked.

She laughed, but a concerned look remained on her face.

"How many do you want?" she asked, as if I were collecting snakes. It's funny the things complete strangers want to know right there in the grocery store.

"We'd like to have as many as we can get," I replied, as if I were collecting treasures.

"Goodness! I have two, and they drive me crazy!" she said. "Two is enough for me!"

"The first two were a challenge for me, too," I agreed. "With the first couple, you are getting all your practice. You are learning to be a parent, and every phase is new. But just like anything else, the more experience you have the easier it gets. I think it's sad that so many people stop at one or two. I've been able to enjoy my last three so much. I have all the joy of parenting, and not as much of the stress. And now that my oldest children are big, I've got some wonderful helpers. I think that many people imagine that having six kids is like having six two-year-olds all at once."

"You look too young to have so many," she said.

"Well they keep me in shape. I don't have time to sit around eating Twinkies and watching soaps," I said.

"So how old are they?" she asked.

"My oldest, Isaac, is seven. Anna is six. Estera is five. Rachel is three, and Naomi is one and a half," I told her, as if rehearsing a poem.

"I bet you are hoping for a boy this time!" she said, keeping a tally of girls versus boys.

"Isaac would love to have a little brother, but I don't mind having a house full of little girls! So I'll be happy no matter what I get."

"Just wait until they are teenagers!" she said.

"I'm really looking forward to that!" I told her. And once again, her eyes got big, her mouth dropped open, and she didn't know quite what to say.

"I had wonderful teenage years!" I continued. "I think my kids will too. Those were the most fun years of my childhood—camping with my family, learning to sew, starting a business, making Thanksgiving dinner, falling in love with my husband . . ."

"Teens are so troubled and sassy these days!" she said. "I guess there's not much you can do about that."

"I know quite a few families with delightful teens, but you do have to make sure they are respectful and well-disciplined from the time they are toddlers. And remember that you reap what you sow," I told her.

"What do you mean?" she asked.

"Well, what happens when you plant weeds in your garden?"

"Weeds grow."

"What happens when you plant flowers?"

"Flowers grow."

"I think it's the same with our children. They are like gardens," I explained. "The parent is the gardener. From the time the children are small, we need to make sure they have plenty of light, pure water, and good nutrition for the heart, body, and spirit. But that's not enough. It's up to us to protect our little gardens from harm. We need to keep out the weeds, the bugs, the dogs, the rocks, the rabbits, and the stomping feet of folks who just want to take short cuts through the garden or steal the fruit."

"I think I know what you mean, but just thinking about the video games my son plays and the buddies he hangs out with . . . you just can't control kids these days. And then with all the junk they pick up at school, I just don't have the time to deal with all of it. You must be a stay at home mom," she concluded.

"Yeah, I am. I've been really blessed to be able to make that choice and have a supportive husband," I told her.

"And I must ask: do you homeschool, too?" She had a knowing look now.

"Yeah, and it's been fun. We've also been able to keep a lot of bugs and weeds out of their gardens this way—plus they get a great education with all that one-on-one attention. And classroom walls and textbooks don't limit us. The whole world is our classroom"

"I just wouldn't have the patience!" she said, smiling.

"Oh, the kids have taught me patience! No one comes by patience without having to learn it the hard way," I confessed.

"What about socialization?" she asked. It's what everyone asked.

"I just don't see the good in having my kids socialize with a large group of kids their own age everyday under the care of just one adult. I think they would pick up a lot of bad habits. But when we are at home, and together in the 'real world,' they get to know people of many ages and from many walks of life. They are best friends with each other, and it helps when your child's best friend is being taught the same morals. That makes everything easier."

"I guess you're right. I never thought about it that way. This gives me a lot to think about," she said. "Well, my ice cream is melting, and ice cream doesn't wait. I need to get going. It was nice meeting you!"

"Nice meeting you, too. I need to get home to all my babies," I said.

"Where are they all by the way?"

"At home playing with Daddy."

"I couldn't imagine my husband taking care of five kids! Well, good luck with the new baby!"

Hope for my Neighbors

This spring I hope you plant flowers. This summer I hope you water them. This spring I hope you take walks. This summer I hope you find a lemonade stand. This spring I hope you turn off the TV and teach a kid how to ride a bike instead. This summer I hope you forget to turn the TV back on because you are too busy enjoying real life.

This spring I hope you find time to fix the screen door and take out the storm windows. This summer I hope you sit out on your porch and wave to neighbours. This spring I hope you plant a little garden. This summer I hope you have enough homegrown tomatoes to bless the whole neighborhood. This spring I hope you start saving a little money. This summer I hope you take a trip to somewhere special.

This spring I hope you learn some new skills. This summer I hope you use those new skills to finish that remodelling project. This spring I hope

you pick up some of the trash in your neighborhood. This summer I hope you get over your littering habit.

This spring I hope you give up fast food. This summer I hope you fit into those jeans you've been holding on to all these years. This spring I hope you prioritize your time. This summer I hope you can spend more time with the ones you love.

This spring I hope you make prayer an important part of your life. This summer I hope you can look back and smile when you realize how God has answered. This spring I hope you clean up the clutter in your yard. This summer I hope you have picnics and parties in it. This spring I hope you say you're sorry. This summer I hope your friendships thrive. This spring I hope you watch the clouds with a child. This summer I hope you watch the stars with your lover.

This spring I hope you celebrate life. This summer I hope you live your life to the fullest.

FIG. 7

WATER BIRTH

It was a Friday night on the first day of autumn, and my sixth child was already overdue. As I slept, I had a dream that two friends were visiting from Korea, and they brought me a large cardboard box. The box was about the size of a dishwasher. They told me to get in the box because it's time for me to have my baby. So I climbed in the box and began having painful contractions every few minutes.

When I woke up from that dream just before midnight, I was still having contractions. The labor pains were coming at about ten minutes apart, so I walked around the house for a while, leaning on the wall during the pain. I waited another hour and a half before waking Josh, just to be sure. I had already called the midwives twice that week for false labor. This time, though, I was pretty sure it was the real thing. At 1:30 am, I finally woke up my husband and told him we better call the midwife again.

Over the phone, the midwife told me to take a warm shower and call her back when I got out to see what effect the shower had on the labor. When I called her back, the pains were coming about five minutes apart. She said she was on her way over to my house.

My mom arrived a few minutes before the midwife. She tidied up the house, lit some candles, and brought me a snack. My husband got out his guitar and played some music, stopping to rub my back during the contractions. I got a little grumpy with him when he didn't put down his guitar fast enough.

After the midwife and her assistant arrived, my contractions slowed down but became stronger. The pains grew more intense as the quiet night continued. I spent some time leaning on the

202

sturdy dining room table. My mom brought me juice, and the midwife rubbed my neck with fragrant oils to help me relax and feel more energized at the same time. She also listened to the baby's heart rate and felt my tummy to check the baby's position. Everything was perfect. The pain got worse. That happened every time. This was my fifth homebirth; the last two babies were born in the kitchen.

This time we had prepared a birth room with a comfy bed, a birth pool, a couch, a handmade wooden cradle, and two small tables. One table held fresh flowers, a candle, a pretty lamp, a Bible, and some snacks. The other table was set up with birth supplies and newborn care items. I had two baskets of baby things ready—one full of boy clothes, the other with girl clothes. Peaceful music played in the background.

In the middle of one especially intense contraction, I hopped into the birth pool, wearing my night gown. My mom and husband prayed for me throughout the night. A few hours passed, and the colors of sunrise flooded in through the bedroom window. A moment later, the older children were all awake and having breakfast. They took turns coming to check on me, comfort me, and ask funny questions. My contractions were very intense but still quite far apart, so I didn't mind visiting with the children in between. They knew that they had to be very quiet whenever mommy started humming.

I would always hum through the pain, and my midwife knew how far along I was by the tone of my humming. I noticed everyone growing excited about mid morning, giving each other knowing nods and smiles. Then my contractions completely changed: they didn't hurt anymore, and I didn't feel up to pushing yet. It almost felt like everything stopped. So I got out of the pool, dried off, and sat down at the table to eat a bowl of Cheerios. We even went out on the front porch to take a few last-chance, pregnant mommy photos by the window.

After a while, my midwife suggested that I try some little pushes during my contractions. So I made a few little grunts, but I was tired of pain, so I didn't try very hard. Eventually, I went back into the birth room, alone with my husband. I was ready to get serious.

"Let's just shut the door," I said with a laugh. " I'll push out the baby and then we can tell everyone to come in and see it." I was half joking. That's when my water broke.

I got back into the in the birth pool and called in the midwife. All the children climbed on the bed to quietly wait and watch. My husband got in the pool with me so he could press on my lower back and help me deliver the baby. Pushing really hurt! My last baby had come in three pushes, but this one was taking more time. I told everyone that I was finished, that I wasn't going to push this baby out because it hurt too much. But then everyone reminded me of how sweet it would be to hold my new baby. They told me not to be afraid of the pain. My mom and husband prayed for me again. I tried about a dozen different pushing positions. My mom suggested that during the next contraction my husband should just pray for me the whole time. He began to pray, and I began to pray in my mind instead of focusing on the pain. At that moment, I had new strength, and the baby began to emerge. The midwife unwrapped the cord, and then I lifted the baby onto my tummy.

The very moment the baby was on my tummy, she pushed up, lifted her head, opened her eyes big and wide, and looked right into my face without a sound. She had a look of wisdom in her eyes. Everyone in the room was amazed. My mom caught this moment on video.

When my husband asked me to check if the baby was a boy or a girl, the child turned its head and looked right at Daddy.

"We have another girl!" I said, smiling. I had a feeling.

Isaac spoke up. "I really wanted a boy. I hope we get a boy next time!" Everyone laughed.

About 10 am, I was tucked into bed to nurse my new little girl. Everyone wanted to see her little fingers and toes. All the older children wanted to feel her soft skin and thick dark hair. She was beautiful, strong, healthy, alert, and content. Nine pounds even, and as sweet as can be. What a precious gift, our little Susannah.

"CAN I HOLD THE BABY?"

I couldn't imagine anything on earth sweeter than holding and snuggling my tiny little girl. She made my heart melt and filled my world with warmth and peace. I just loved having a tiny little baby in my arms. But there was something else I also loved: the joy that my one-week-old baby brought to everyone else who got a chance to hold her. The most-used phrase in my home that first week after she was born was, "Can I hold the baby?"

My mom was one of the first people to hold little Susannah, and I know that a million memories were flooding into her heart. "She looks just like one of my babies! I think that this one is going to look like you!" she said. Then she told me the stories about when I was tiny.

I loved watching Josh hold the baby, too. It reminded me of the day we met back in 1991 at the church picnic when he held my friend's one-month-old baby and I decided I'd marry him someday. I loved putting each of our new babies into my husband's arms. Here we were with our sixth child, Susannah. The world seemed to stop spinning, and the sun shone a little brighter as I watched him look into her sweet baby face.

Isaac fell in love with his new little sister. He carried her into church on Sunday morning, pride and joy radiating from his smile. My own heart melted a little, too. He's learned to bounce her just right to keep her happy. And one day, he held her in the grocery store when our family went shopping. Rachel was riding in the shopping cart, little Naomi was in my husband's backpack, and I needed my hands free to shop. Isaac beamed as baby Susannah slept in his arms.

My dad held little Susannah for the first time on a day I was having trouble getting her to sleep. It took Granddad less than a minute to lull her into bliss. My dad has a way with babies, and with each new grandchild I place in his arms, my heart melts all over again. I have a picture of my Dad back in 1976 with a big bushy beard and a hippie shirt on. I am in the picture, too, cuddled in His arms. He had that same look of pride holding Susannah— it's the same look I saw on Isaac's face as he held the new baby.

My older sister, Charity, stopped by to visit and held the baby five times. One afternoon, she sat in the rocking chair beside the window, gazing into Susannah's tiny face for the longest time. This was the first new baby in the family since Charity's three-year-old little boy went to heaven. Our whole family was learning anew how precious life is and what a gift each little child is. Holding a newborn brought comfort and healing to her broken heart.

One morning after breakfast, our little Naomi, just one-and-a-half years old, disappeared for a few minutes. As soon as I noticed she was missing, my husband rushed into the room where the baby was sleeping. The baby was still sleeping peacefully, only in Naomi's arms instead of the crib. Naomi was all smiles, and she was holding the baby "just like mommy."

On Saturday night when Susannah was one-week-old, five young friends stopped by, girls who mostly came from broken homes and hung around our house regularly looking for the love and attention they were missing at home. They couldn't hold the baby long enough, each gazing into her face and stroking her silky hair. They peeled back her blankets and nightgown to peek at her tiny fingers and toes. They would have stayed all night, taking turns holding the baby.

With each new child, the love somehow multiplied. The love of our family was like a fire, and every heart held a candle. With each new baby, the glow of life, the warmth of love, the light of a hundred smiles, the laughter, snuggles, and kisses multiplied. The joy of living filled the air and brightened up the world for everyone who came to our house.

THE RESCUE

A sad string of heart-breaking events brought my dear friend Melanie to our door. She had just moved back to Indiana from Montana with a baby in her arms and three little children by her side. She was a single mom now, living in a hotel, and she had no car.

Life couldn't be much worse, but as she told me her story, the love of God flowed from her heart, and I saw a rare and unusual faith. She had been forsaken by her husband but not by Jesus. She was confident that He would provide for her, protect her, and help her through. She spoke of forgiveness and grace when most women would be fuming with bitterness and hate.

Over the next few months, she and her children spent many days with our family. We gave her our extra car, and she helped me with babysitting and helping in our home while I was weak from morning sickness. Eventually, she moved into a vacant parsonage and started a daycare in her new home.

One Friday afternoon in early fall, Melanie was going to babysit the older kids while Josh and I snuck off for a weekend in the hills of Brown County—the same area where we spent the first few days of our honeymoon years before. As soon as we pulled into her driveway, the kids all ran into the house excited to play with their friends and see the new kittens. We piled the coats and backpacks on the dining room table. Melanie told the kids that it was tomato-picking time and was about to help everyone get their coats back on when I remembered something I needed to give Melanie that had been left in the car.

The two of us carried our babies outside, and as I rummaged through the back seat looking for the missing item, we heard an explosive sound coming from the street. A car had wrecked in front of the house, and a tire flew off and was spinning across her yard at lightening speed. The tire slammed into the house, breaking a window. We ran back inside, terrified of what we might find.

The house was quiet, and the tire was in the middle of the dining room table that had been flipped over and smashed to pieces. The kids' coats were covered in theshards of glass that had been blasted into the dining room, living room, and kitchen. But where were the children?

Only Isaac was downstairs, sitting on the couch a few feet from the broken glass. He was safe. We found all the other children safe in the attic looking at the kittens. When we had left the house just a minute before the accident, all of the children were in the dining room, preparing to go back outside. But apparently Aiden and Faith had invited the girls to go upstairs to see the kittens just as we walked out. Rachel had been left alone in the dining room but ran upstairs just seconds before the tire came flying through the window. We all prayed and thanked God for keeping everyone safe, and then we started cleaning up. I called Josh, and he came right over to help. We changed our plans for the weekend.

Later that evening, Rachel came to me and said, "Mommy, where is Aiden's daddy?"

I looked into her big blue eyes, trying to figure out how to tell such a sad story to a three year old. "Aiden's daddy is far away."

"No, he's not! Aiden's daddy was here!" Rachel insisted. " Where is he now? He's a nice daddy. He told me to go upstairs fast when the tire was gonna come in the window. So I obeyed."

Rachel wasn't wondering why Aiden's daddy left them. She had just assumed that the angel who saved her from the flying tire must have been the man of the house.

THE GOATS ON MAIN STREET

For more than seven years, Josh and I tried to find a way to move back out of town and further into the country again—we wanted to be more self-sufficient. We had tried three different times to get our Simpler Times Village off the ground with dreams of a sustainable rural village surrounded by friends and family with the same vision. Just as we were planning to break ground on our last attempt, the housing market crashed. We lost our investments, went into debt, and disappointed hundreds of families who wanted to live in the new community. We were on the brink of fulfilling a great dream, but when winter of 2007 came, all of our plans fell apart. We struggled not to become discouraged, but we felt like our family of nine was stuck living in the big Victorian house in our rundown, Midwestern town.

"I want to live what we believe," Josh had told me one day. "But I just don't see how we can live our dreams without getting out of this town. The economy is in the toilet. We can't sell the house for what we put into it. Gas prices are headed for $4 a gallon. We have a baby due in April."

"I want out of this town so bad, too," I said. "When I come into the driveway, I just don't have that 'I'm home' feeling. I was at the Apple Family Farm yesterday picking up milk and eggs, and I just wanted to stay longer and listen to the sound of the hens and the bells on the cows. I saw the sunset—I can't see the sunset from our porch."

"We need to live what we believe, no matter where we live," Josh declared. "In the spring, we are going to homestead. We can build raised bed gardens here; we can get a couple dairy goats and laying hens. We'll put in a wood burning stove for heat next winter, and plant grapes, berries . . ."

"And fruit trees?" I asked.

"And fruit trees," he said.

In my heart, I hesitated to believe that we could really do it all on Main Street. I tried to have hope, but I was afraid. Things hadn't worked out for us that year. Our dreams had come crashing down. I looked at my husband, so thankful that through it all our love for each other had stayed so strong. Hard times had come, but we had built our life together on solid ground. We stood on the front porch, and a gentle snow began to fall as blue light flickered in the neighbor's windows. "I really do want a goat," I murmured. "Josh, are we on the wrong planet?"

"This world is not our home. We are only passing through," he reminded me, smiling.

"So, what if we do everything we ever dreamed of in this house, and then we sell it?" I asked.

"Maybe we need to be content to stay," he replied. "It's a bad time to sell."

"I want to be content. But I really want freedom to have sheep, goats and chickens again. Am I crazy?"

"Yeah. But that's why I fell in love with you," he said.

Spring brought with it our new baby girl, Laura—our seventh child. My mom came to stay with us for a few weeks to help with the children. We also took the "For Sale" sign out of the yard and decided it was time to start making all our dreams come true right where we were in the yellow house on Main Street. We had just received our first economic stimulus check from President George Bush. In all our dreaming, we spent that money five times before the check finally arrived! When it did come, though, we used the money to create a sustainable urban homestead. There were now two dairy goats and eight laying hens in the backyard. We had fresh milk and eggs in the fridge, and by the time Laura was two weeks old, my mom and husband had built 16 raised bed gardens and planted 14 fruit trees. Until that spring, we had never really put our whole hearts into living life to the fullest in the yellow house on Main Street.

One afternoon when the weather had warmed, I held my new baby and looked out over the gardens, listening to the clucking of the hens and the happy voices of all my children. I felt at home at last but still wondered if I was on the wrong planet, especially when a police officer showed up at our doorstep and told us that our animals were not allowed in town limits. He showed us a law: "Certain farm animals are prohibited in Fortville, Indiana: cows, chickens, pigs, horses, and bees."

I smiled. "Okay, we'll get rid of the chickens right away," I told him. "But I don't see ducks and goats on that list."

He read the law again and agreed with my observations. "Well, I guess you'll have to take that argument up to Town Hall."

And so we did. The goats were here to stay, but we started thinking more seriously again about moving to the country.

A Visitor to the Urban Farm

If you were to visit our home, you would have trouble finding a spot to park. We turned half of the driveway into raised bed gardens last spring. On your way to the front door, you might have to navigate a jungle of bicycles, strollers, skateboards, and gardening tools. The bunny on the porch will wiggle his nose, and you will have to be careful not to trip over the colorful collection of shoes by the front door.

Ring the doorbell and half a dozen children will curiously peek out the windows to see who's visiting. As you wait for me to come to the door, a chorus of children will chime in about all the details. "It's a man and a lady, she has a yellow shirt and pink lipstick. The man doesn't have any hair. He's got a green jacket. They have a gray car—it looks like grandma's car but different. Can I show them my goat Mommy? Do they have presents for us? Does that lady have gum in her purse?"

As I open the door, four children will dash out and maybe a pet goat, too. The children will all hop on their bikes and go zooming up and down the sidewalk in front of the house while we talk. The child that wanted to show off her goat will help catch the funny critter before she eats the neighbor's flowers. Another child might run into the backyard and grab a pet duck to show off.

After all of the excitement, you might even forget why you came. My husband will want you to see the new wood-burning stove he just installed, and then he will tell you about all the great bargains he found on Craig's List. Then he'll say, "I'm sure glad you showed up. Would you mind helping me stack all this firewood?" No one will ask you why you came, but they might offer you some homemade goodies or homegrown produce.

You will get a tour of the gardens, and the little ones will tell you about the fruit trees we planted the week that baby Laura was born. While you help the children pick strawberries along the side of the house, you will hear stories about how baby Laura was born at home while daddy played music on his guitar and mommy was eating strawberries.

If you are interested, I might teach you a lesson on how to create a complete biodynamic ecosystem in the backyard. Before you leave, my son will want to give you a tour of the mini-farm that we manage five blocks away. It's right on the edge of town. I hope you like animals... and children.

flowers

original piece

roots

Potato plant

We would all walk to the farm together, and my nine year old would talk with you about politics, economics, the Revolutionary War, and the Great Depression. You might wonder to yourself if this boy is going to grow up to be the Governor someday. And then someone will ask you if you want to milk a goat. By this point, you might not only forget why you came, you might also forget what year it is and what planet you are on.

As you drive away, I'll turn to my husband and say, "Honey? Who were those nice people?"

And he will look at me and say, "I thought that you invited them."

"Nope. I never saw them in my life," I'll add, as we will laugh to ourselves and finish stacking the firewood.

CHAOS AND CONFESSION

One night that summer, I stayed up past midnight trying to solve all of life's troubles and mysteries. The chocolate Isaac had brought home from the parade earlier in the day was gone; I ate it all. I was anxious and worried. Where were we headed? Where was God leading us?

The next morning, I woke up sleep deprived with a candy hangover. My plan was to get out of bed just long enough to help my husband get the kids dressed for church. After putting in my contact lenses, I looked around in disbelief. I hadn't heard any tornado sirens, but it seemed obvious that something had blown through this house with a vengeance. Or maybe it was just the children.

Three of my kids were up before the light of the sun streamed through the windows. That explained it. Apparently someone had decided to make a bath just for the toilet paper rolls. Someone else—or maybe the same person—put the fruit basket in the bathroom. Three little people had already changed clothes about thirty times that morning. The mountain of laundry that had been on the dining room table when I went to bed the night before was on the floor, and it looked like the one year old made her own breakfast. To make matters worse, my husband made his own breakfast, too.

My baby girl spit up all over me, and all my clothes smelled like sour milk. My husband even recommended that I go buy myself some pretty pajamas because I looked like I was wearing the shower curtain. I found prunes in unusual places around the house. Dozens of buttons from the laptop keyboard were on the living room floor. And the one year old tried to change her own poopie diaper.

After Laura was born that spring, my plan had been to take time off from normal life to rest and recover. Josh couldn't take time off from work to take over the mommy role, though, and with a baby in my arms, six small children to care for, and a new homestead to run, rest really wasn't an option. I was exhausted.

After my brief inventory that morning, I told everyone to go back to bed. When they didn't, I did. Eventually, the house quieted again except for the 80s rock coming out of the stereo, not my choice for Sunday morning music.

A BETTER DAY

The following morning, I woke to the sweetest words: "My wife, my lover, my friend." Josh whispered to me, and I snuggled up closer to him. He kissed my forehead.

"Friend," I said sleepily, smiling. He called me his friend. He loved being with me, sharing a life, a home, a family, a mission, and a thousand dreams.

I closed my eyes once more as he stroked my cheek, and I wondered, *How is it that I am so loved? How is it that I am so happy? How is it that my heart is so full of delight as I wake up every morning? How is it that my heart is so full of peace as I fall asleep beside my husband in this room with yellow walls, in this house with seven children, in this marriage of ten years, in this Victorian home on Main Street?*

I pulled my feather blanket up to my chin, thankful for its warmth, knowing that just being warm this morning was a gift to be grateful for. *How is it that my husband is more in love with me than ever, even after 17 years? How has he become my dearest friend? And why do I feel as if I am breathing the air of heaven right here on earth?*

That morning, sunlight did not fill our room like other mornings. Rain was falling outside our windows, and the air was chilly and fresh. Some mornings I felt like I was waking up on the wrong planet. That morning felt just like home should.

One by one the children came to greet me with their morning exclamations. Baby Laura was still sleeping on my chest when Josh had woken me with his sweet words. Now, Laura's blue eyes blinked, then opened wide. She smiled. Who needed sunshine when baby Laura was in the room? She whispered

"Da-da," and two hearts melted, as her daddy swooped her into his arms and climbed out of bed.

A few moments later, little Susannah, now two years old, pitter-pattered into our room, climbed up into the big bed, snuggled under the warm covers, and said "Twinkle Star?" We spent the next five minutes singing "Twinkle, Twinkle Little Star," just the two of us, while the sounds of morning echoed through the house.

Josh was up and had already fetched some Joe's O's for baby Laura. Now I could hear him calling to the children upstairs. "I'm making bacon and eggs, and none of you are going to eat until your rooms are clean and the beds are made," he said. The kids were excited about breakfast. We had bacon only about once a year, and Daddy had done the shopping the night before. He was proud to bring home organic, uncured bacon he had bought on sale.

Naomi, our three year old, usually cooked the eggs. She would go out into the backyard and hunt for the duck eggs herself— the ducks were always finding new spots for their nests. The only help Naomi needed was turning on the stove. She also was known to round up the goat, bring her to the milking stand on the back porch, and milk her. But only if there was no milk in the refrigerator. Helping in the kitchen was Naomi's joy. Lately, she had been insisting on washing the dishes, too. Anna our oldest daughter was eight that summer and was the next child to appear on the scene.

"Dad! Rachel is doing it again! She told me that she needs to take a little rest before she helps clean the room, and she won't help me!" she said, tattling on her sister.

"Rachel! Come down here!" Josh called.

Little Susannah began hopping on the bed, asking to sing "Twinkle Star" again and again and again.

Daddy interrupted Susannah's song to tell me that the mice stole the cheese from the mousetrap. "The cheap traps work better, but this new kind is much easier to set," he said. Then he was gone, back to the kitchen, and Susannah and I were singing again.

"Hi there, little Frog," I heard my husband say.

"Daddy! I'm not a frog. I'm a turtle!" seven-year-old Estera proclaimed.

"Okay, little Turtle. Do you know where Susie's clean clothes are? Go upstairs and pick out an outfit for your sister," he told her. She headed off.

"Good morning, Isaac, sleepy-head." I heard my husband's voice once again as our nine-year-old son joined the morning buzz around the house. "Put on your shoes; you need to bring up the trash cans. Oh, and we are out of firewood."

"Daddy!" Anna yelled, "There's a mouse in this trap! Mom! Come here quick! Mommmmm!"

I climbed out of bed to join the family and see last night's catch. A fat little mouse, indeed.

"Don't touch it, Naomi!" Anna ordered, in her best mommy voice. "Now go wash your hands!"

As usual, the floor was feeling a little "crunchy" under my feet. I had a feeling someone had gotten into the sugar. I began looking for my shoes but couldn't find them, so I grabbed Isaac's hiking boots instead. I was amazed that I wore the same size shoes as my nine-year-old son. Wasn't he just a baby? Then he walked in the room, muddy foot prints behind him, a load of firewood in his arms, and a proud smile on his face. He was wearing my shoes!

My husband smiled at the chaos all around us and kissed me again as he handed Susannah a banana, not noticing that she already had one. "Two! Two Nananas!" Susannah cheered. The house was bursting with life, laughter, and chaos, and my husband took my hand and drew me to a quieter corner of the house to kiss me longer, to shower me with the comfort and passion of a man still deeply in love with his bride.

THE UNEXPECTED EVACUATION

The house was quiet early on a chilly morning later that year. Snow was falling and winter was creeping in through the hundred-year-old windows. Our seven children were still sleeping, and my husband had just returned to bed after putting a few logs on the fire. Suddenly, the doorbell rang, followed by hard knocking.

"Who could that be? The sun's barely up?" Josh said, quickly grabbing yesterday's clothes. We concluded that our goats must have gotten loose and were running through the neighborhood. I mentally prepared to jump out of bed and chase our crazy goats through town.

When Josh got to the door, however, a construction worker was standing there.

"Sorry to bother you," he said, "but we are going to be digging in your driveway, and we need you to park your car down the street. We're putting in the new sewer line."

While Josh moved the car, several of the younger children came down wrapped up in blankets and huddled near the woodstove. The older children didn't get out of bed. The baby called from her crib. Josh was taking the trash to the curb but came in for a coat. "It must be ten degrees outside!" he said.

I decided a hot breakfast would be nice. Just as I started boiling water for the oatmeal, Josh ran into the house shouting, "Grab the kids and run to the park! The guys just busted the gas line fifteen feet from the house. This could be really bad!"

The smell of gas was filling the air.

About five minutes later, I was standing in the snow at the park with seven shivering children. I was terrified as my husband went back to get the car—at least it was down the street a bit. I looked toward our home, wondering if the gas would ignite and send our corner of the neighborhood up in flames. Then, I turned to focus on the children.

I had grabbed a pile of clothes and blankets and mismatched shoes. The kids were crying as I tried to sort out the shoes and socks. I was still in my pajamas and had given my own coat and shoes to one of the kids. The babies needed diaper changes, and there were not enough shoes to go around. Two children had no pants on because they had been rushed out of bed. The big kids held the little ones as we waited for Josh to come with the car. One of the children had a bad scratch from climbing through the bushes, and we were all freezing and hungry. To top it all off, I had morning sickness and was beginning to feel dizzy and nauseous. We were unprepared.

A few minutes later, Josh arrived safely with the car, and we all piled in and drove out of town. We didn't even have a car seat for the baby; we hadn't had time. We were told that the street would be closed for several hours, and it was unsafe to return to our house until further notice.

Where would we go, with no car seat, no diapers, and not enough shoes—and I was still in my pajamas? Besides that, we had friends coming in from out of town. They would arrive in about an hour, and we didn't have their phone number with us. I don't think we even had our wallets.

We found refuge at Josh's parent's house. They were in Florida, but we were able to stay a few hours at their house. Thankfully they were prepared for us, and they didn't even know it. They had a dresser full of children's clothing. They had diapers and snacks. I borrowed clothes too, and the children played with the toys in grandpa's toy box. We were able to use their computer to search for our friend's phone numbers.

As we waited for clearance to return to our home, we prayed together, thanking God for His protection and wondering if our neighborhood had burst into flames. Josh found a Bible and read to us from Proverbs 14: "In the fear of the Lord there is strong confidence, and His children will have a place of refuge. The fear of the Lord is a Fountain of Life, to turn one away from the snares of death."

We prayed for God to protect our home, and He did. When we returned later that day, all was well.

CAFÉ WEDNESDAY

Almost a year later, I was sitting in a bookstore cafe on a Wednesday morning in early September, sipping a sweet mocha. Josh was back at our new house with the kids overseeing "Art Day." The kids all had new sketch pads, and they were happy to draw pictures all day.

I was sitting at a table by the window enjoying the peace. The colors there felt good to me; the music was calm and jazzy. Josh had known I needed a little get away after the night I had had. I had trouble falling asleep and kept waking up off and on. Actually, it was just another normal night for a woman due to have a baby born any minute.

The month before, we finally moved to the country and were living in a little blue rental house surrounded by forests and fields on the edge of the Apple Family Farm. We were trying again to sell our big yellow house on Main Street, a house that could no longer hold all of our dreams. We were ready for a change, so we planted a "For Sale" sign in the front yard and tried to keep the house clean for the showings.

It was hard to keep the house clean and in order and ready for buyers with seven children running around. When a friend told us about a house in the country that we could rent right away, we decided to make the move. We loved all the land, and we immediately bought a dozen sheep, a dozen goats, a dozen chickens, and a dozen ducks. I am not sure how many cats were living there, but we counted two big white dogs, only one of them belonged to us. We were living a dream, but paying rent for one house and a mortgage on another wasn't going to work for long. So we prayed for our yellow house to sell, with hopes of buying the country house in the future.

I made pancakes and cooked up some omelets made from duck eggs for breakfast that morning before I left. The chickens had stopped laying eggs, and we didn't know why. Estera washed the dishes, and then Isaac made a second batch of pancakes for himself and Josh. I searched in the laundry basket for a pair of socks for Susie and found a kitten instead. Isaac said he just found a kitten, too, sleeping in the trash can.

Anna had gone out early to the pasture and was running with the dogs, playing with the goats, and watching the sheep. Susie got her shoes on just in time to go out to the field with us, holding daddy's hand as we walked. Anna was all smiles when she saw us coming because a new lamb had been born and was already dancing around her mama's legs to everyone's delight. Rachel fed the rabbits and the hens with this morning's table scraps. I hoped they all liked pancakes.

As I sat in the cafe thinking about all my children, my heart filled with love and awe. Each child was so unique. Isaac loved to cook. He was ten, then. Anna loved to climb trees. She was nine. Estera loved to draw animals. She was eight. Rachel loved to swing. She was six that year. And Naomi loved to draw pictures of flying sheep; she was four. Susie loved to wash the dishes, and I loved it, too. She was only two. And Laura? Laura simply loved her shoes and socks. She was one. Oh, and everyone loved the kittens.

As I looked out the window, I didn't see the parking lot, the cars, and all the people dashing here and there as I expected. Instead, I saw the sky, and I felt the responsibility of teaching and training all these children. My heart filled with a prayer for my family.

"I dedicate myself to teaching my children to follow after You. I want to give them the tools they need to grow in many skills. Help me not to waste time on things that have no value.

Please give me Your wisdom to know how to spend their time; childhood is precious and fleeting. As I teach them help me to give each child a unique education that prepares them for Your calling on each of their lives."

Sarah's Journal

Tomorrow

Tomorrow, I want to paint my walls with hills and trees, butterflies and clouds, and sing the songs from "The Sound of Music." Tomorrow I want to ignore the laundry and play outside with my toddlers. I want to be close to creation. I want to feel the wind and the rain and watch the sky.

Tomorrow, I want to bring fresh milk from the barn and fresh flowers to the table, and let my little ones feel the joy of gathering a basket of fresh eggs. I want to look out the window and watch the neighbor's horses run. I want to share my two year old's amazement as we examine the beans sprouting in a jar on the windowsill. I want to build Lego towers, block towers, and couch pillow towers . . . again and again and again. I want to watch with wonder as my baby falls asleep to Mozart. Tomorrow, I want to drink a cup of loose-leaf tea and share a cup with a friend as we talk about the treasures we found at garage sales. I want to fill my house with used books and take time to read them. I want to learn all about the way my great grandmothers lived, and teach those skills to others. I want to make things I couldn't buy and make other things anyway. I want to make my home an expression of creativity, discovery, and faith, and I want my heart to be an expression of Jesus.

Tomorrow, I want to listen to the hearts of my children and be the one who nurtures them from sunrise to sunset and all through the night. I want to giggle with my daughters and read about tractors with my son. I want to smile when people tell me that I must have my hands full—smile knowing that my hands are full of blessings.

Tomorrow, I want my husband to come home to joy, to peace, and to unconditional love. I want to kiss him and rub his back if he's achy. I want him to enjoy a meal seasoned with herbs from our garden. I want to sit on the porch swing with him and watch the sunset and seasons change. I want to listen as he talks about his work and all the new people he meets then talk about making plans for our next big adventure.

Tomorrow, I want to say yes to the things that matter most and say no to the things that stand in the way of peace. I want simplicity. I want to live by faith. I want my neighbors to see a candle burning in the window but never the blue glow of a television set. I want to be thankful and content with what I have, and when I have more than what I need, I want to give. I want to give even when I must sacrifice.
Tomorrow night, I want to fall asleep in a room with wood floors, open windows, and soft yellow walls as my husband reads the Bible to me. I want to dream big dreams, and then make them come true . . . in my own back yard or on the other side of the sea.

Tomorrow, I want to wake up in my husband's arms and listen as he prays for our family. And I really want to live my life like I was designed to live it. I want music, purity, sunlight, and the laughter of children. I want to know the one who made me. I want to make God smile. I guess what I really want is for tomorrow to be a lot like today.

BIRTHDAY BABY BOY

Even though the baby in my womb was my eighth child, as I got close to the day of his birth, the miracle of his life amazed me as though he were my first. A new child was about to be born. A son.

I opened my Bible to the book of Romans, and my eyes fell on chapter 12, verses one and two. They became my prayer.

Oh Lord, I present my body a living sacrifice, holy and acceptable. I will worship You as I offer my body to be used by You, the Holy Creator, as You bring forth my little son. I am ready to hold my new baby.

Fill me, Lord, with power by your Holy Spirit to receive from You Your power, comfort, peace, and calm as You speak to my child to come. Lord, be near to me, hold my hand, and bring me your peace. Let my soul be still in Your presence. Draw me close to Your heart. Let me know that your arms are around me as I release this child from within.

May he be strong, and may I be strong. Lord I dedicate this child to You. I commit his days, his breath, his heartbeat, his being into Your hands. Let Your work on earth be done through this child.

Let him know You from his youth. Let him be wise, kind, compassionate, and just. Give him great wisdom and understanding. May he be a light in the world as he walks in purity and truth. May the beauty of his heart and soul point many to Jesus.

Help him to bring justice to our nation. Help him to discern the truth and bring glory to You in his life's work. Let him be a peacemaker who brings unrighteousness to light. May he make music to you. May he speak Your Word to others. May he be like Joseph and David. Let his life be a fragrant offering to You.

Pour out upon him the love of all his family. Pour out upon him Your grace and glory. May he often hear Your voice. Let him hear You loud and clear in his heart and mind.

Bless him with gifts of Your Spirit. Bless him with power and grace to help others. Bless him with a keen mind and great love for learning. Empower him to serve Jesus in wonderful and mysterious ways. Use him for Your glory, honor, and praise. Oh Lord, I am so thankful for the gift of being a mother to this precious child. Lord, I submit myself to you, and I give You my body to release this child into your hands.

I gave my husband a baby boy on his 31st birthday. I wanted to name the baby Luke, but it was Josh's birthday, so I encouraged him to name his little son. It took him only a minute to decide that he wanted to name our new son after his dad, Joseph. Since this was Isaac's first brother, we let him choose Joseph's middle name.

So, our ten-pound boy, our eighth child, born on September 21, was called Joseph Arrow Brown.

Mommy, Write My Story!

One morning, three-year-old Laura woke up with the sun and wanted to tell me her good dream.

"Mommy, get your computer and write my story," she said. So I typed her story, word for word.

When I grow up, I'm going to have two shops. I will have a cookie shop and an ice cream shop. I will have a pink and purple car. I will have chocolate chip cookies in my cookie shop, lots of them. Do you like that kind? I will sell chocolate chip ice cream too, like my cookies.

I will have a baby with purple, yellow, red, green, and yellow dresses, beautiful dresses, and a big Rapunzel Dress. I will play, "Where's my baby? Peek-a-boo!"

I will be so tall to reach my chocolate, way up high so no one else can get it. I will give my baby a little half. I will give my big kids big halves. I will give my kids their own chips and candy—I'm a good mommy. I'll buy candy.

Okay, now. My husband will be a big daddy, so big, he can reach my chocolate, too. I'll share it with him. My house is going to be colorful—pink and red and purple and yellow. I'll have some chocolate in my house. I'll have a bunny for my kids, two bunnies for two little kids. I'll have some kittens for my big kids, and they will be so happy.

I'll have a car and two horses. I'll go to the farm to get milk, goat milk. Mom you can ride on my purple horse, and I will ride the pink one. You will be a big, big grandma, and you can drive my car. It will be so fun.

I will be the mom, and you will come to my cookie shop, and I will talk to you about my babies, and you will have chocolate, too. The dad will go to work, but I'll stay home at my house with two tiny babies and lots of big kids and two little kids. That's all I need. The grandma can go work at my shop. I'll take care of the babies. You can go talk to my husband at the shop. Dad will be the grandpa; he will go to work with his car. I'm going to go on vacation. My car will have batteries to go all the way to Florida. My batteries will die in the car, and somebody will fix my car and put gas in it to go to Florida. I'm going to go hiking with my dad when I'm a mom. I'll be jumping over things when there's pokey stuff. I'll go to the beach, and there will be jellyfish on the sand that don't sting. Now, I'm gonna have a big, big house. BIG mom! I think that's all ... oh but I will have big panties, and I will go to the ocean, and I will have contacts.

When it's raining and thunderstorming, we will go in the house. I will let my kids outside when it's snowing; it will be snowing. We will all build a snowman with my kids. I will have hot chocolate.

When it's my birthday, there will be big rocks falling; the big rocks will drop on people from the sky, and Jesus will save the people. It will be scary. Jesus will come. Jesus will be so happy, and the rocks will be gone. The people will go to the hospital. My house is strong; the rocks won't hurt my house. My kids will be in the house, so safe. When the rocks are gone, we can go outside, but there will be little rocks, but they won't hurt my house.

After the rocks go away, I'll have an apple tree and a pear tree. There will be rain, but no thunderstorm, just rain. Here will be a huge tree as big as my house. It will be a colorful pear tree. My husband will be really happy when I paint my tree. My husband will say, "You can paint all your trees."

It's a good dream, but the part about the rocks is not a good dream, but Jesus made it good because He saved the people from the rocks. And we will say «Thank you to Jesus!» On my next birthday there will be no rocks, just snow, beautiful white snow. I'll get two chocolate bunnies from my two little kids. Ok, now, I'll have toys from my babies. I'll have big animals from the pet shop.

"Is that all?" I asked when she grew quiet.

"Okay, that's all," she said. "That's all I have, Mom."

PART 4

CROSSING OCEANS

Returning to Main Street

A "For Sale" sign caught my eye, and it happened to be in my own front yard. I looked at the sign; I looked at the big yellow house. I looked at the faces of the children piled into our green Suburban as we pulled into the driveway. Then, I looked at my husband. Our life in the country was over, we were moving back to Main Street.

"So, are we really home?" I asked.

"I guess so," he said.

"So can I take down the sign?" I asked.

"If you want to," Josh replied.

And that was that. As I stood in the slushy snow yanking on that crooked sign, I had a feeling of relief, sadness, hope—then peace. It was like taking a breath of cold, winter air. It was the closing ceremony of the dream we had a chance to live, even if just for a season.

Last summer, I had stood on the front porch of our little rented farmhouse, tossing scraps to my flock of free-range hens. My son brought in a pail of fresh milk from his dairy goats. My little girls gathered flowers in the meadow just beyond the front door and made forts in the woods on our hillside. Newborn lambs called to their mothers. And my pet ducks came at the sound of my call. There were ripe tomatoes to pick, and hundreds of birdhouse gourds grew bigger everyday, much to my toddler's delight. Our second son was born in that house as the last rain of summer fell pattering on the metal roof. But as summer gave way to fall and fall turned to winter, it became clear that we could not stay.

A truck zoomed by, splashing muddy, slushy snow in my direction and bringing me back to the reality of life on a busy street in our small, Midwestern town. This town. I once had so much hope for this town. I wanted to raise my family here. I wanted to live my dreams here. I wanted to help bring people together to revitalize the historic neighborhoods. I had visions of festivals in the park. In my dreams, I heard the music of village life and hoped to plant more flowers, grow more trees, and touch the lives of the people around me.

I hoped for a rural community that would hold on to its timeless roots even as it took on the advancement of suburbia. I wanted to see new businesses coming and staying—not coming and going. I wanted to invite the next generation into my home and give them some reasons to love their hometown and reasons to stay. For seven years, I gave my heart to this town, and I discovered a community of kind and gracious people, hardworking, full of hope and faith. Just the kind of people who have what it takes to breathe new life into a community.

But over time, I also came to realize that this was a town full of people hushed and timid under the thumb of a grumpy and poorly managed local government. That same government often came knocking at my own door, knocking down our trees, knocking down our dreams, and stepping on our liberties. No one wanted to rock the boat because we all knew that the ones who did ended up with dented reputations. We wanted to stand up for what we believed in, but we often had to endure many harsh and ugly words from a few loud and angry people. Those loud and angry people were few and far between, but they barked the loudest, and they tried to bark my family right out of town.

When we moved away to our farmhouse in the country, we were sad to go. I felt like I was leaving behind so many people

I had come to love, so much work undone, so many gardens unplanted, so many teens with nothing to do and no reason to stay, so many dreams and ideas just sketches in my plan books. But how could I give my children the life I hoped for them in a place like this? And how can a girl like me with plans and big ideas get anything done under the thumb of the not-so-good ole boys?

In many ways, it was nice to have a chance to be free, living on a dirt road with no neighbors in sight, no one to hear my chickens clucking, no one to complain about my silly old goats, no one to tell me I can't sell soap and candles to my neighbors. But no neighbors also meant no one to bake muffins for, no one to play chess with, no one to plant gardens with or trade cookbooks with. No neighbors meant no one to invite to a backyard picnic, and no children climbing over our fence and knocking at our door. No neighbors stopped by our house to tell us that the bunny was loose again. There were no shops down the street to walk to, no parks to play baseball in, no teenagers sitting on our porch for informal art or music lessons. No village life. No community.

We were always trying to live a dream that left us feeling like we were on the wrong planet, but we came back anyway, back to Fortville. After some time away, coming back seemed right. I missed my neighbors, my friends, my park, my town, my sidewalk, and my front porch. I missed writing stories in the newspaper, and I missed telling stories to the kids who knocked on my front door.

With spring just around the corner, we couldn't help but dream new dreams for the work we would do in this town. We had flowers to plant, murals to paint, apologies to make, and friendships to build. When I yanked out that "For Sale" sign, one dream faded but a bigger dream still shone in my heart. We wanted to pour our hearts into making the town a better place.

New Vision for an Old Town

One day as Josh was reading the local newspaper, he called me over to look at something. It was almost time for local elections, and there was an open seat on the Town Council. We had joked about running for town council, just to rock the boat and bring fresh vision to the old town, but Josh was busy with work and I was busy having babies. Besides that, neither of us had a good chance at winning, since it was unheard of for anyone to be elected without first being born into one of the "political" families in town.

As we continued looking at the new article, though, something tugged at our hearts, and I encouraged Josh to go ahead and sign up for the election. "Not me!" he said, "I think you should do it! Everyone loves your column in the weekly paper, well almost everyone, and they know you."

So that year, I ran for a seat on the Town Council and surprised everyone when I won the election. I couldn't believe how hundreds of people in the town wanted my political signs in their front yards. Three other great people ran for the same seat, but the people of Fortville chose me to represent them. It was an honor to serve the community, and I was even appointed vice president.

Since we were really investing our lives in Fortville, Josh opened a computer shop on Main Street and business went well, though the costs of owning a store and hiring employees ended up being a bigger investment than we realized. Josh was busy running the shop and was always exhausted at the end of the day. I was lonely and even started playing Farmville late at night to pass the time while waiting for Josh to come home. We were going in so many directions until my sister Charity moved to Fortville and came to work for Josh as a store manager. After many years of feeling distant from my sisters, it was so much fun to share life again with Charity and my nieces.

Our roots were going deeper and becoming more entwined with others in our town every day. I was busy being the vice president of the Council with eight children to raise, festivals to plan, neighborhoods to beautify, problems to solve, meetings to attend, police officers to hire, and emails to answer. Oh, and a garden of my own to plant. Sometimes, I found myself in too deep with everything going on, so my sister jumped right in and began to not only bail me out but also fill my life with her love and energy.

Together, we worked to organize community events, and we watched the streets come alive with festivals, talent shows, princess pageants, car shows, fundraisers, and cake decorating contests. We saw the crowning of the Snowflake Princess and participated in the first lighting of Main Street in December 2010. Charity was with me rain or shine. We rejoiced together as we watched the town become less of a bedroom community and more like a village. Josh and I could hardly get time alone during that busy season as we dedicated ourselves to running a store, managing a town, and revitalizing Historic Main Street. We watched how our work was blessed; many people were coming out of the woodwork to volunteer and serve in the community. The town began to come alive again; it was like lighting a match. In the year after Josh opened his shop on Main Street, many other stores appeared: an ice cream shop, a café, gift shops, a gun shop, a horse shop, a pet grooming business, and a couple of new restaurants.

But in the midst of all the excitement, Charity also encouraged me to slow down. She knew that I needed to make changes for the sake of my marriage and family. She could see that the good things happening in the town were wearing on my most important relationships.

A couple of years passed, and as spring turned to summer, Josh and I drove down the street, smiling at the people walking by, amazed at all the changes that had happened in such a short time. We went to lunch at one of the new cafes and looked into each other's eyes. We talked about how crazy life had become, how this wasn't the life we always wanted to live. As happy as we were for all that was going on, we had a feeling that our work was finished in that town. Josh took both of my hands in his and began to pray for God to show us the way out.

When he finished, he looked up at me. "Sarah, what is it that we both agree on?" he asked. "What is it that we both really want to do with our life?"

It took less than a minute to remember that we were called to the mission field, and we both agreed that it was time to say goodbye to Fortville, Indiana. It was time to say goodbye to our family and to the American soil where we had both lived most of our lives, where our children had lived theirs. It was time to take whatever steps we needed to take to bring our family to a better place where we could fulfill our calling together.

Painting My Vision for Main Street

Paintings by Sarah J. Brown depicting her ideas for revitalizing downtown Fortville, IN

DYSLEXIA

Isaac started reading at age three. Back then, I thought homeschooling was going to be easy. Anna, our second child, was born dancing, drawing, and dreaming, but at age nine she was still reversing letters and forgetting how to sound out three-letter words. She continued to struggle with pencil and paper, and I didn't know why. I had started both children with the same reading program, but Anna wasn't learning to read.

I tried several reading programs over the years, but nothing helped. Nothing interested her. Reading was exhausting and confusing. I really began to feel like there was something wrong with her, and because we were homeschooling, I blamed myself. I was afraid to talk to anyone about Anna's problem with reading. I never suspected dyslexia. I just thought I was a bad teacher until Estera, our third, taught herself to read and write at age five. She would always play school with the workbooks that Anna couldn't use. By then, we had dozens of them.

One fall day a couple of years earlier, Anna and I were sitting under the big tree in the backyard working on reading lesson number one for the 30th time. I was still trying to help her see the difference between b and d. We were making a new set of colorful flash cards but seeing no progress.

She looked at me with tears in her eyes. «Mom, there is NO difference! I will never read!" she said. "Can't I just be an artist and a mommy when I grow up?» I remembered having the same dream when I was a little girl and the same struggles. I had blamed the school system for my problems with reading, but Anna was being homeschooled, how could the same thing be happening to her?

I looked up into the sky and asked God to show me how to help my child. The first thing I realized was that I didn't have what it takes to help her and needed to seek out a professional. I had to get over my own fear and pride and ask for help. The first reading tutor we hired was mystified by Anna's problem too, but we eventually found a specialist who understood Anna. The teacher evaluated Anna and revealed that she had dyslexia.

Now that our problem had a name, I spent the following year researching dyslexia. I learned that children with dyslexia tend to be bright, inquisitive, and creative. They are thinkers, dreamers, inventors, artists, and dancers. Like Anna! Like me! They also need to touch, taste, feel, experience, and manipulate things in order to learn. They think in pictures, movies, music, feelings, and movement. They are full of talent, but often feel slow, stupid, different, and misunderstood.

I learned that dyslexia is so much more than a learning disability related to reading and writing. Dyslexia is a gift. As a parent with a dyslexic child, I had the responsibility to provide my child with the encouragement, education, and tools to become who she was meant to be. So I tried everything that the experts recommended—well everything that we could afford. But nothing really seemed to help her with reading. That's when I finally gave up.

"Okay Anna, you can be an artist,» I told her.

I took her to the art store and bought her everything she wanted; she was in heaven. Day after day she created beautiful works of art. She even won a national art contest. Every morning when the other kids would sit at the table with their workbooks, Anna would spread out all her art supplies and sing little tunes while she worked for hours and hours. I knew that she was in her element doing what she was designed to do. But I really did believe in my heart that she needed to learn to read, and I knew that it couldn't happen the normal way.

One morning I was looking over her shoulder as she finished a beautiful portrait of a woman dressed like a character from a Jane Austin book. I watched as she signed her name like a four year old. «God?» I prayed. «Show me how to use art to teach Anna how to read and write. I know that You want her to be able to read the Bible someday. I know that You know everything. I know that You answer prayers. Please show me how to teach Anna to read.»

A few days later I had an idea. I sat down next to Anna and began to draw a series of little faces. Happy, sad, happy, sad . . . «Anna, what comes next?» I asked.

I handed her the pen. She completed the pattern. Perfectly, of course—it was art. For the next hour, I played this little art game with her. I would draw a series of pictures, and she would complete the patterns. She thought we were just playing a fun little game, but I had a plan.

Eventually I began putting symbols, letters, and numbers into these artistic patterns and drawings. I wanted to see if including the letters in the art would somehow help her stop reversing the letters. Logic told me that she would never be able to move on to reading until she stopped confusing her letters. I felt like she needed to relearn the letters in the context of art. I believed the creative part of her mind could be tricked into reading without confusion, without reversals, without tears.

At first Anna didn't even notice that the patterns included letters and numbers. To Anna, the symbols were part of the cool design. I watched with amazement as she drew the lowercase bs and ds without any hesitation or reversals. Eventually, I added whole words to the art and patterns. At first the words were isolated from their meanings, but over time, the words became meaningful and had pictures with them. She began reading those words as if she had been reading all along. Next, I added phrases, sentences, familiar rhymes, and Bible verses. She didn't even hesitate. The confusion was gone.

Two months later, my nine-year-old daughter was reading comic books and following recipes. She was writing emails, entertaining herself with chapter books, and eventually reading from the Bible. She also continued to develop her artistic talents with dreams of illustrating books for kids along with her sister.

As Josh and I looked at our life and remembered our dreams, we once again heard the calling on our hearts to let go of all the things that were keeping our feet on American soil and follow Jesus into the unknown. We had always wanted to raise our children on the mission field, but though we sought to go, the doors were always closed. But life was changing, and an open door was set before us. People sometimes tend to think that children will hold you back from serving God with your whole life, that having a child with disabilities would certainly mean that there is no hope of fulfilling any other calling. With God all things are possible, though. He used my daughter's learning disability to enable our family to answer God's call upon our life to help others. And through this method we discovered to help Anna overcome dyslexia, many children around the world would soon learn to read.

Sarah's Journal

Dyslexia

Over the years of telling Anna's story, I discovered that many parents just like me struggled to help their dyslexic children. I had no idea that about 10% of children have symptoms of dyslexia! Many parents felt like school was failing their child, or even worse, that they were failing their child as parents. Often fear and pride keep them from seeking help.

I wanted to help. So I began creating the drawing games that worked for Anna for other teachers and parents to try with their dyslexic children. I watched with joy as children just like my daughter learned to read by using my drawing and logic games. My little games became popular, so I created and published two sets of activity books for dyslexic children. We called the program Dyslexia Games; kids called it fun. Now, I am currently helping over two thousand children who are using the program and loving it! Best of all, children who once struggled with bs and ds and couldn't even read three-letter words are now reading with confidence!

Teaching Anna to read was one of my greatest struggles as a mother. I couldn't understand why God would allow a child to struggle with reading since I knew that He wanted her to be able to read the Bible someday. But all this was part of God's great plan. He knew that I had a dream years ago to create interesting curriculum for children, but I gave up that dream when I followed the call to missions. I let go of my plans to go to college to learn to produce educational books for children when I said yes to a semester in Hungary to help a family with their children. God not only gave me the desire of my heart, but over time, the sale of these books was able to replace my husband's job, allowing our whole family the new freedom to live anywhere on earth with an internet connection.

Draw the missing parts of each picture and complete each word.

Eagle

agl

My Adventurous Husband

In 2010, life was still very full, even though we had been looking for ways to simplify life. The phone would not stop ringing, and Josh was working crazy hours. One day, Josh said that he was always late because he knew that life was short and he wanted to pack as much as possible into every day. He didn't see any value in taking time between all of life's "happening moments."

But there I was, longing for a different pace. I wanted to slow down, rest, adjust, warm up, ponder, be quiet, watch, learn, and listen.

He wants to hike the Appalachian Trail.
He would leave these shores today to raise a sail.
He will play his music in a foreign land.
He'll pitch a tent, light a fire, hold my hand.

He wants to see the stars from mountaintops.
He wouldn't miss a sunset or a late night talk.
He promised me the Redwoods and the Western coast.
He'll pitch a tent, light a fire, hold me close.

He wants to have a picnic every afternoon.
He wouldn't mind another baby sometime soon.
He wants to laugh, love, smile, climb a tree,
He'll pitch a tent, light a fire, sing with me.

He wants to tell the world His Good News.
He'll be outside whenever the sky is blue.
He wants to share life's great adventures with me.
He'll pitch a tent, light a fire, living free.

He's led me to a dozen foreign shores.
He plans to bring me to a dozen more.
He'll help the kids build castles in the sand.
He'll pitch a tent, light a fire, hold my hand.

It seemed like Josh didn't sit still unless he had a seat belt on. His to-do list was a mile long, and he was always doing something. He gets a lot done! But I felt like I couldn't keep up with him. I found contentment in knowing that though he seems easily distracted and loves to start a new adventure at every opportunity, I was and always will be his favorite distraction. Wherever he goes, he wants to hold my hand.

Joseph's Orphan House

Early in the summer of 2012, we began to talk more seriously about our desire to be missionaries, often including the children in those discussions. We started reading books about missionaries to them and began to pray about where to go. The first real step was getting passports for everyone, although we didn't know where or when we would leave on our journey. We also took the final steps to create our online business, www.DyslexiaGames.com, which would support our family anywhere in the world. What seemed like an impossible dream, suddenly was within our reach. By the end of August, we had over four hundred students using our new Dyslexia Therapy. The business was becoming viable.

One morning we placed a jar on the breakfast table and filled it with little slips of paper. Every day after breakfast, as the sun shone in our window, we would pull the papers out of the jar. Each one had the name of a country, and we prayed for the people there, asking the Lord to lead us to the place he was calling us. We prayed for Liberia, Romania, Ukraine, Austria, Jamaica, St. Kitts, and a few others. The kids were all willing to go, even two-year-old Joseph.

While I was cleaning the kitchen one night, little Joseph walked in with a flashlight, climbed up on the kitchen counter, and said, «Mom, when I grow up like Daddy, I am going to be a big missionary with a hammer, two drills, and a screwdriver.» Then he went on to explain the details: «I'm gonna fix the orphan house with the saw, and I'm gonna tell people about Jesus. Yeah, it's really cool. That's right. I'm gonna have a Bible and tell people about it. Jesus has a big job for me.»

Later when I was tucking him in, Joseph told me he was going to bring a mom and a dad to the orphan kids. The next morning at the breakfast table, he told the whole family about his "good dream» of being a big man with lots of tools and building an orphan house. He said he would bring enough tools for the orphans, and he would teach them how to build, too.

In the afternoon when we were at the park, Joseph started talking about his dream again. He also wanted to build a playground and a church for the orphans. With all the seriousness and confidence of a little boy who is about to turn three, he told me that he *would* get some daddies for the orphan babies. He said he would have a big guitar like Daddy and sing songs with them. He said he would teach them to sing, «Jesus Draw Me Close» and «Jesus Loves the Little Children."

One night a few days later when I was reading my Bible, Joseph came into my room. "Hi Joseph! I'm reading my Bible. When I read my Bible, Jesus talks to me," I explained.

He smiled and plopped down beside me. "Jesus talks to me, too," he said, not missing a beat. "He came in my room. He was working on a chair, a little chair for the orphans, and he showed me his tools. He told me four things. He would always be with me. He would always be in my heart. He said he had a big job for me to do. And I am going to build an orphan house!"

The whole family caught Joseph's vision for orphans, and we began to pray about going somewhere where we could help orphans. We were willing to stop living the American Dream and start living a new life. We began to sell things, give things away, and simplify. We began to plan. We began to let go of everything familiar, not knowing where we were going but willing to follow God's calling together as a family.

As time passed, we began to feel led to start in Italy. Though we had been studying the Bible for 20 years, Josh had never attended a Bible college. For a long time, he had wanted to devote a season in life to learning the Bible on a deeper level so that he could be better prepared to teach others. We also felt a special connection with the Italian people after our last two trips there. We were ready to move to Italy, get involved with the local Calvary Chapel, share the love of Jesus with the people we would meet, and prepare for a future as missionaries. We didn't know how our desire to help orphans fit into our plan to move to Italy, but we knew that this was going to be our first step, a step of faith. We had an ocean to cross.

Sarah's Journal

A House with Open Doors

We have a house of fourteen rooms and six computer screens.
We have two big refrigerators, to hold our food and drinks.
We have a van filled up with gas. We are full and rich and fat.
We whine and gripe, we grasp for more, and toss it in the trash.

We go to church three times a week, to grow closer to God.
We give a little, take a lot, and talk about the lost.
The widow and the orphan they rarely come to mind.
The hungry, poor and fatherless, we'll feed some other time.

What does it mean, my Lord and King, to be your hands and feet?
Does it not mean that I must give myself to those who weep?
What does it mean, my Savior Christ, to love the way you do?
You call me to lay down my life, to love them as you do.

Children cry and parents die for lack of food and water.
You say to take the orphaned ones to be our sons and daughters.
Lost, alone, and wondering, for a crust of bread they grasp,
They seek and search for things of worth, among discarded trash.

I'd trade my house of fourteen rooms for a house across the sea,
And fill that home will little ones who need God's touch of peace.
Bring in the orphans, widows, the hungry, weak, and poor.
I'll trade my house of fourteen rooms for one with open doors.

Give me a house of healing, a house of peace and rest.
Open up the windows, let all who come be blessed.
Free us from this western world to set up camp across the sea,
You call us now, my Lord and King, to be your hands and feet.

Come wind, come rain, come bumpy trains, we'll take the dusty trails
knowing you did not complain when you endured the nails.
We don't have much, but all we are, we offer up to you.
We'll bring your hope to those in need, to love them as you do.

MOVING TO ITALY

I woke up early enough one morning to watch the first rays of sunlight illuminate the sky over Montebelluna, Italy. The church bells ringing through the small city announced that it was 6 am. I looked out from one of the tallest buildings in the town center. From a window in the seventh floor flat where we were staying, I saw rooftops, a clear sky, and the shadowy mountains that outlined the horizon all around. What was once a calling, promise, and relentless desire to follow the Lord to a new land was now a reality, with an address.

Just weeks earlier, we had little more than a vision for missions, a heart for Northern Italy, four plane tickets, a map, an invitation from a few missionaries that we had never met, a place to stay, and just enough extra money in the bank for a rental car. With 70 families praying for our journey, we said goodbye to six of our children to spend 10 days in Italy.

I always had a feeling that my next baby would be born it Italy. I had faith that some missionaries would be moving away and we would step in to fill their home and ministry before winter. As fall approached and my December due date drew near, Josh and I pondered these things in our hearts, knowing that it was humanly impossible but also believing that with God all things are possible. There were many questions: how, when, where? But knowing the One who made the earth, the sky, the sunrise, and the shadowy mountains, it wasn't so hard to believe that He would be able to put His plan for our family into action.

Things still looked impossible a few days into our scouting trip, but then, just as we had hoped, God moved.

A few weeks earlier, I had prayed that if God really wanted us to move that He would provide money for 10 plane tickets, visas, rent, and moving costs before we signed any papers—about $15,000. And we needed it in three weeks' time so that we would have everything we needed to make the move. That was far more than we had ever seen come in from Josh's sales job and our Dyslexia Games business. But as we searched for a home in Montebelluna, it was clear that God was providing. Our total income for the three weeks prior added up to exactly $15,000, and we had been out of the country for 10 days of that span with little time to work. The money just rolled in; we had just enough for the plane tickets, the visas, the rent, and the moving costs.

We also learned that some missionaries had recently moved away, and their home right in the heart of Montebelluna would be available. A day later, Josh took a big step of faith and withdrew enough money from the bank to pay the first month's rent. The house wasn't quite big enough to be a long-term fit for our family, but it was a good place to start. We registered with the Italian government and set up an appointment for 3:30 to sign a contract for our new home. The landlady joyfully signed the papers, excited that her seven-year-old niece would have a bunch of little girls next door to play with. We planned to move in on November 1, 2012.

That morning before we left to sign the contract, we had received an email—an email I will never forget. It was one of those clear signs from God that only people like George Mueller or George Markey might get. It was a letter from a missionary on the other side of Italy, a homeschooling mom with four children. She said she had been praying for us all morning, and she had a picture in her mind over and over of a big truck showing up at her house, and her family loading all their furnishings and belongings into the truck . . . for us. She had had no idea why she was seeing this in her mind, or if we needed anything at all. She didn't have any idea that we were signing a rental contact that very afternoon for a home with no furniture, dishes, beds, books, tables, or lamps. She didn't know we were planning to move in on November 1st. But as it turned out, her family was moving away on November 1st, and though they didn't know where they were going, they felt like God wanted us to have nearly all their household possessions.

Needless to say, it was with great confidence in the plan and power of the Lord that we had paid our first month's rent. At the signing, the landlady asked what we would be doing about furnishings, and she was among the first to hear the story of how God had provided. We told the other missionaries about how God was providing, and they offered to go to Turino to pick up our stuff. The landlady said we could begin moving the furnishings into the home at any time.

Looking out over our soon-to-be-home early that morning, it was good to recall again the miracles of the past couple of days. We would need the assurance God gave us to energize us for all that was ahead in the coming weeks. Even that very day was to be a long one for us. We planned to fly out of Venice that evening, spend seventeen hours in Paris, and arrive home the following evening just before midnight. Before we left, Josh would lead worship and morning devotions for a group of students from all over the world who were also in this city attending Calvary Chapel Bible College. Later, we would gather all the paperwork for our visas before packing for our long trip home.

Anna and Isaac were there with us as we laid the groundwork to return with the whole family. As we paid rent on a new home, they asked an obvious question about our old one: "what are we going to do with our house in Fortville?"

"Let's just watch and see what God has planned," we told them. "We have many needs, many questions, and a lot of work before us. But we have a great God, great friends, and a lot of people praying for us. This is clearly God's work, not ours. God knows we need to rent or sell our house in Fortville."

God also knew that I was six months pregnant and needed help packing. He knew we needed to sell our van, to find homes for our pets, and to give away or sell nearly all the household possessions we had collected over the past fourteen years of our marriage. God had given us everything we needed right when we needed it, and as we headed back to Fortville, He even gave us His peace.

Once we were home, things happened quickly, and friends gathered around to help. My friend Candace came to our house every week to teach our family Italian. My friend Leslie made plans to travel with us to Italy to help with the kids on the flight over and help us unpack. Amber and Aaron began praying about getting passports to visit. And other friends opened their homes to our pets. My midwife, who had delivered five of my children, made plans to fly to Italy to deliver my baby in December. Everything was working together in beautiful ways. So we bought one-way tickets and received Italian visas that would allow us to stay for a year.

What more could we do but trust in the Lord and follow the path as He illuminated the way, as He brightened up the morning sky, as He called us to come, as He called us to go. We had just a month to say goodbye as the sun set on one adventure and rose in all its wonder, beauty, and glory on the next.

FELTRE

Sarah's Journal

Passing the Paintbrush

When I travel, I've learned to pack light, yet I've also learned to make room for a few bottles of paint and a single, perfect paintbrush. It's become my habit to pass along a mural where once the walls were blank. I have painted kitchens, baby's rooms, orphanages, churches, nursing homes, ice cream shops, and even a whole town.

As I paint, someone is always watching me, often a child. I see them with a wistful look in their eyes, and I know that within this child is an artist waiting to be drawn out. They might surprise me with a cautious, "Are you a real artist?" or the precious declaration, "I am an artist, too!" Adults often confide in me, "I love art, but I could never do this." Or maybe they remember, "As a child I was always drawing" or "I always wanted to be an artist, but I'm not very talented." That is when I pass them my paintbrush, remembering what it was like to be an eleven year old watching my mother paint and wishing for a chance to try.

First, I allow them to do the easy parts, and then I show them how to do the detail work. At first we work together, then I give them their own part of the wall. If my new apprentice stays with me until the mural is finished, I will show her how to wash the paintbrush and then I let her keep it, along with the leftover paints.

It is my passion to multiply my blessings wherever I go, by sharing my gifts with others.

I pray that my art and imagination would extend into every facet of my life because I have a vision for passing along this blessing that God has given me. I always wanted to become an artist, but my life currently is filled more with a string of airports, train stations, mother-daughter talks, long walks, cooking pots, water births, Facebook posts, and trolley rides than time to paint. I'm always on my way to some place new and have very little time for creating art, unless I'm arranging a colorful salad or braiding a little girl's hair. Once in a while, I still find time to paint a mural. Now, God is always bringing new people into my world, or bringing me into part of someone else's world. And I want to take what I have and share it with others. What do I have? Love for children and a love for creativity. What I have I will give.

I have left many murals behind me, but my calling is not to paint, my calling is to pass my paintbrush.

A Day in Italy
By Anna Brown, age 12

The last day of 2012 was a bright and sunny day. Our new baby was only two weeks old, and mom thought it was a good day for an adventure. She was tired of being stuck in the apartment after having the baby. So five of us wanted to go sightseeing, and five of us wanted to go shopping, and the baby ... well she just wanted to eat, sleep, and poop!

We decided to take a train to IKEA, a big store that sells lamps, beds, pillows, furniture and much, much more. On our way there we had to run to the train station (because we have no car here in Italy). It seems like we are always running to train stations lately. We got to the station just in time to catch the train. We also were thinking about going to Castle Franco, an old walled city that surrounds an ancient village with a real castle. So on the way to IKEA, we stopped at Castle Franco. On our walk to the village, we took lots of pictures of amazing old buildings, pigeons, and doorknobs.

When we arrived in the village, a little outdoor market was going on in the town center. We had fun looking at all the different things that were for sale, but all we bought was a bag of apples. They were some of the best apples I ever tasted!

Next, we went to a small grocery store where dad bought everything we would need for a picnic. We were looking for a grassy place to eat our lunch when dad saw a fish market, or shall I say he smelled a fish market! Mom and most of the kids did not want to go in because it smelled so bad! So dad, Rachel, and I went in; we are the brave ones in the family. It smelled so gross! They had dead fish with the eyeballs still attached! They also had crabs, squid, octopus, clams, lobsters, and all kinds of gross stuff I had never seen before! I almost fainted it smelled so bad! We finally left after Dad looked around for a while.

We found an amazing spot to eat our lunch on the stone bridge at the entrance of a huge castle. There are castles all over Italy, and they are so beautiful. This one had a real moat around it. What a place to eat ham sandwiches, chips, popcorn, cookies, and cheese! Of course we shared our lunch with the ducks and geese swimming around in the moat under the bridge. And then the pigeons joined the party, too. Mom was busy nursing the baby, and Dad was busy talking about the fish shop, so they didn't notice that we shared every bit of crust and most of the popcorn with the birds.

Mom was tired after lunch, so she and I and the baby went to a pretty little café. Dad and the rest of the kids explored around the castle. Mom and I each had a cappuccino. We got back on the train after a few hours to go to IKEA. The train brought us to Padova where we had to take a bus. After a while, we realized we were on the wrong bus! This happens to our family all the time! As always, we eventually got on the on the right one! The bus had handles hanging from the ceiling. I'll admit that Esther and I got a little crazy, but we were just practicing gymnastics! The little kids joined in, and that's when Mom got mad and made us all hold on to the yellow bar instead. Dad didn't even notice. I think he was still talking to mom about the fish shop!

When we got to IKEA, it was about to close, and we had to shop quickly. Each of the kids had 20 Euros to spend. I bought a lamp, bed desk, and a pillow. Esther bought a pillow and lamp, and all the little kids got huge stuffed animals. Mom warned us not to buy more then we could carry. We should have taken her advice! You should have seen us on the buses and trains on the way home. Mom and Dad ended up lugging seven big bags of stuff, along with nine fussy, whiny, tired kids all the way home. Well actually only eight of the kids were fussy; I was a perfect angel!

HOUSE HUNTERS INTERNATIONAL

While we were in the process of moving to Italy, Josh and I were contacted by one of the producers of the HGTV show *House Hunters International.* The producers wanted to film our adventure for their show. At first I thought the offer was some kind of scam, but it wasn't. They were serious. Friends and strangers had often asked us when our family of 11 would be on reality TV. We used to laugh, but not anymore. Our episode ran during the winter of 2013.

In October, we had sold the 15-passenger van, received visas, had a goodbye party, rented out our house in Indiana, packed up half a ton of luggage, and boarded an airplane. We crossed the ocean while we were sleeping. We arrived in Italy on November 1st, the day our lease started on our new home. Baby Ember was born six weeks later.

We lived in that first apartment in Montebelluna for a few months, but even when we signed the lease, we knew it wasn't big enough to be a long-term home for our family. By spring, we were ready to go house hunting again. This time we had our hearts set on a house on a hill with green shutters, just outside Montebelluna.

The *House Hunters International* crew met us at the train station and followed us around Montebelluna for four days of filming. They recorded our family dragging half a ton of luggage out of the train station. They videotaped the kids eating gelato, an Italian ice cream. They filmed the whole family shopping at the Italian farmer's market, signing up for library cards, and going out for pizza at a sidewalk cafe. They even got to see our new kittens.

Though we had already chosen the house we wanted and in fact, had already moved in, that was no problem for House Hunters. That was where reality met TV magic—they simply asked us to reenact our house hunting experience. There was a lot of pretending. They sent movers into our house to make most of the furniture disappear and rearrange the things they didn't feel like moving. Representatives from the show introduced our family to a local realtor, and then the film crew followed us around while we looked at some really interesting homes. All of the homes were on hills, and they all had green shutters and amazing views. One of the houses was originally built in the year 500. Another of the houses was the one we were already living in.

The director of the show had about a hundred interview questions to catch on film. We did most of the interviews outside with beautiful Italian vistas all around. We had to stop the filming every time a dog barked, a car passed, a helicopter flew over, or a tractor passed by. They asked us questions like, "How did you and Josh meet?" "Why Italy?" "How do the kids feel about the move?" "What are the most important features you are looking for in a home?" and "Is there anything that you and Josh don't agree on?" They filmed from morning to evening, keeping the kids happy with gelato and keeping me happy with cappuccinos and lattes. As we answered question after question about our lives and why we had moved to Italy, we were reminded of all that had happened in our lives to bring us to the point of boarding a plane and crossing the ocean with nine children, the littlest one inside. Faith. Risk. Adventure. Love. Courage. Destiny.

The kids loved learning about how reality shows were made, and since we were homeschooling, this was a great opportunity for them to get some hands-on experience in filmmaking. Isaac, who was 14 by that time, hung out with the film and sound crews, asking the guys at least a hundred of his own questions each day about creating documentaries. After the experience, Isaac planned to create his own reality show about his little sisters and brother called, *Will They Eat It?*" a cooking comedy for kids and parents.

I never thought I would be a television actress. I had given up on that idea when I ended my modeling career at age 15. And I didn't like the idea of being fake. But we were in front of the cameras, and we believed that it was in God's heart to lead us to this interesting opportunity. We prayed that our lives would inspire people that we would never meet and challenge them to follow their own callings and enjoy life with their children. It bothered us that the producers were changing the story to make it fit into their format, but TV is TV, and we gave it our best.

THE REAL REALITY SHOW

At the end of our *House Hunters International* episode, the producers included clips of our actual lives—no more pretending. There we were, a family of 11 in our house with green shutters on a hill in a small Italian village. Our lives were full of music, laughter, and fun as we gathered around our big table or played games in the living room. This was the real reality show we lived every day in Montebelluna.

On most days, 12-year-old Estera would wake up first—she's the early bird. She loved to cook, so she always prepared breakfast and brought me a cup of tea to start the day. She would do her online schoolwork before the other kids even woke up. At 8:20, Estera would let everyone know that breakfast would be served in ten minutes.

After we all had breakfast together, our family would all gather in the living room, and Josh would bring his guitar and Bible. We would sing some songs and then read the Bible together. The four oldest children each would read a few verses. Then, we all would talk about our favorite parts of the Bible story and pray, asking God to bless our day and our loved ones.

If it wasn't raining, my husband would take the little children to the park on Tuesdays and Thursdays, and the rest of us would head off to music lessons or the public library. Sometimes, we would clean the house and then take the train to the mountains or a nearby historic town. On most days, we would just stay home. The children who were eight years old and older would spend time studying before lunch.

At the end of the day, we would gather for dinner—a dinner prepared by one of the children—and then Josh would tuck in the little children. He would tell them stories and sings songs to them. While he tucked in the little ones, the older girls would help me clean the house, and then we would make tea and sit in the living room in our pajamas. Isaac would study in the evenings on the computer. I would read aloud from a novel for about an hour. Sometimes I would have trouble putting the book down and saying goodnight.

After the kids were in bed, Josh and I would enjoy the quiet of the evening, knowing that we have had life to the fullest and survived another amazing day as the parents of nine children.

One particular day, I woke up to the sound of roosters crowing and church bells ringing out my window. I also heard children yelling down the hall, and before I could put in my contacts, I heard three sides of the story. We had stayed up too late last night and didn't set an alarm clock. Now, the milk was spilled before I had a chance to make it to the breakfast table.

"Girls! Stop screaming! You are going to wake everyone up," I said, trying to hush my angry daughters.

"Mom, no one is sleeping except Isaac, and he needs to get up anyway!" Estera explained, as the sound of chaos echoed in the hallways. Why was everyone up so early?

I put in my contacts, picked up the baby, and found one of my slippers before I arrived in the dining room. Seven little people and only one cereal box. Laura, the five year old, was pouring her own milk. The familiar feeling of smashed cereal gritted beneath my one bare foot as I removed Joseph, the bouncing four year old, from the table top. He was wearing a bicycle helmet, a towel for a cape, and Speedos over his pants. He sported unmatched winter gloves, a slipper on one foot, and a boot on the other. Like all boys his age, he was swinging two swords.

"Everyone back to bed!" I shouted. Seven little faces turned my way puzzled and amused.

"We are going to start over with this day!" I explained. "I'm going to clean up this mess, and we are all going to pretend like this day never happened. In a few minutes, I will call you down for breakfast. Now go back to bed!"

And so we started over. With two slippers on my feet and courage to face a new day, I watched the children disappear up the stairs, all except for one. Anna, my oldest daughter, remained at the table with a look of guilt on her face. I paused; we met eyes.

"Okay Mom, it's like this," she said, taking a deep breath. "I'm really sorry. I ate your chocolate last night, and I'm really sorry. So I won't ask you to get me anymore right now. But can you get me that kind of chocolate in the green wrapper for Christmas? It was so good. But really, I'm sorry."

I forgave her, handed her the baby, and sent her to her room. I quickly cleared the messy table and reset it as Josh picked up his guitar and plopped down on the couch. It was a new day—all was quiet again except for the peaceful music and a whispered prayer.

Sometimes I just need new beginnings. It could be as simple as sending the children back to bed and resetting the table, or something more complicated, like moving our family across the ocean.

At 9 am, my call echoed down the halls: "Good morning everyone! Get up and come down for breakfast!"

A minute later, a flock of happy children gathered around the table. Even Isaac showed up, having slept through the first beginning. He never knew that for the rest of us this was our second time at the breakfast table. Josh laid down the guitar and smiled at me. A familiar prayer, ten amens, a second chance to spill the milk. It was a day with two beginnings, and the second was better than the first.

After breakfast, we all gathered in the living room. Josh picked up his guitar again, and a room full of happy little voices sang along. After a few songs, Josh read from his Bible and prayed for each of the children and me, too. A few minutes later, everyone scattered—some to do the cleaning, some to work on school projects, some to search for lost shoes, and some (or one) to swing swords and chase the cat.

I helped Josh get the four youngest children ready for a trip in to town. We have no car, and we often walk a few miles with the kids when it's time to do the shopping, go to the library, or play at the park. My plan was to sit on the couch with my laptop and work for a couple of hours and help the older kids with homeschooling. After lunch, I would walk into town to work.

A WALK WITH GOD

The sun broke through the clouds for a moment to warm me as I walked down the hill peacefully. Our year in Italy was almost over. I had just returned from a visit to Ukraine to visit my mom and dad, a visit that included trips to orphanages. My parents left America a few months after we did. My dad was teaching at a seminary in the city of L'viv, and my mom was busy learning the languages and helping with orphans. They had invited us to join them in Ukraine—maybe permanently—and the open door beckoned us on.

As I walked, each new gust of wind seemed a little colder and I wished for a scarf and gloves. It had been a long time since I walked a mile without a little hand to hold or a stroller to push, without a teen to talk to or a husband to dream with. I didn't like the feeling of being alone until I remembered that God was still with me. So I talked to Him as if He were walking with me, His wonder filling my thoughts as my peace was renewed.

I passed a mother coming up the hill with one child skipping along and one sleeping in the stroller. She looked tired. As she passed by, I realized that I, too, had become so busy managing life and its responsibility that I had begun to have fewer conversations with God throughout the days. When I was younger, I had a running conversation all day long with the One who was always beside me. But over time, I began to pray only when I could get a quiet moment or really needed help. I came to God in prayer as if I were having a meeting with my boss, having coffee with a friend, or calling my dad on the phone. How could I forget that God was always near, ready to listen, ready to help me, ready to give me peace and hold my hand every minute of every day?

So as I walked down the hill, I began again to turn my thoughts to God. I began again to bask in His promises, His gifts, and His blessings. As the warm November sun broke through the chill of the air and yellow leaves crunched under my feet, I began to feel the presence of God again. My quiet prayer became a new song in my heart.

As I entered the city, everything was unusually quiet and still except for the endless rush of autumn leaves dancing on the breeze. I reached in my pocket for my shopping list when I remembered that it was only 3 pm. All of the stores were still closed for the daily siesta. I would have to wait for the shops to reopen after 3:30. I needed to buy a few things for my mom. Josh would be flying to Ukraine the following morning, and I wanted to send some things Mom couldn't buy in Eastern Europe.

Though the streets were quiet, all of the cafes were open, so I stopped in for a glass of fresh-squeezed orange juice and a pastry. I brought my Bible with me, and I pulled out my blank book to begin writing, but I had forgotten to bring a pen. Without it, I couldn't even write "pen" on my shopping list. So I just used the time to read God's words of comfort, and as I read, courage poured into my soul like my glass of fresh-squeezed juice.

The church bells began ringing at 3:30 to tell the city it was time to get back to work, but I stayed a little longer, enjoying the promises that filled my life with hope. I had been a little fearful lately, knowing that everything was about to change, knowing that our time in Italy would soon be a memory. The next day, Josh would be house-hunting in L'Viv, and I would be at home alone with all nine children, waiting to hear news and see pictures, waiting to find out if Josh felt like our next adventure would be in Ukraine. I wished we could go together.

An hour later, I finished the shopping and decided to find another café now that I had a pen and could sit down and write a little. The streets of Montebelluna were alive again as I picked a café—there were so many to choose from. I ended up at one that doubles as a candy shop. Anna had eaten my chocolate the night before, and I was beginning to miss it. A little chocolate and a latte macchiato would do the trick.

It was sunset when I finally walked back up the hill. When I came into the house, it was quieter than usual. Anna met me at the door, but dashed upstairs before I had a chance to say "hello." Josh was busy packing in the living room. Ember, now 11 months old, was toddling around the room happy to be on her feet. Susie, Laura, and Naomi were sitting at the table painting with watercolors. Joseph was climbing on top of the table still dressed in his astronaut costume, though now with two matching slippers. He still had on the towel, the helmet, and the speedos, and he was still swinging two swords in his hands. I grabbed him before he had a chance to step in the paints.

A burst of giggles echoed through the halls, the kind of giggling that sounds more dangerous than silence coming from a room full of girls.

"Anna! Estera! Rachel! Come here right now! What are you doing?" I called.

Silence. The kind of silence that sounds more dangerous than a chorus of mischievous giggles.

"Girls! Come down here right now!" I demanded.

"Mom, we were just painting!" Anna called out from the top of the stairs.

"And?"

"And Esther painted a cat," Rachel added.

"On paper?"

"On my face. Don't worry, Mom. It's washable, I think," Anna said.

Three girls appeared at the bottom of the stairs with colorful faces and bashful smiles. They were so cute. The little girls looked at the big girls. "Please, Mom, can we get our faces painted too? Please? Please?"

Joseph walked into the room and looked at the painted faces. "Can you make me a superhero, too? Please?"

"Sorry kids, it's bedtime!" I said. "Daddy will come up stairs to tuck you in. Go brush your teeth."

It took Josh a little longer than he thought to finish packing, and by the time he got upstairs to tuck the little girls in, they had all been turned into painted kitties.

I could hear Anna singing, her songs echoed down the hall until she appeared in the doorway, Ember grinning and giggling in her arms.

"Mom, Ember's walking now, and she can say a lot of words," Anna said. "She tries to do everything we do. She's growing out of all her tiny baby stuff. How long exactly does it take to get another baby?"

"About nine months," I reply, mindlessly.

"Okay, 'cause Ember needs a baby sister," Anna said before she plopped Ember into my arms and disappeared down the hall. As the last few minutes of nighttime chatter filled the air, I did a little math in my head, wondering if I might begin to feel waves of nausea around this time next month. I would wait a little longer before spending any money on an expensive Italian pregnancy test.

I smiled to myself as Ember wiggled out of my arms and dashed out of the room. Josh scooped her up on his way upstairs to tuck in the little kids. A few minutes later, a young man stepped into the living room. He looked very familiar—a lot like Isaac used to but taller. I noticed that my son had my eyes and my husband's smile.

"Mom?" he said. "Are there any leftovers? That chicken and rice glop was really good!"

Before I could answer Isaac, Estera fluttered into the room. "Mom? Have you seen the cat?" she asked. "It's my turn to sleep with the cat."

Before I could recall where I last saw the cat, Rachel appeared in the crowded doorway. "Mom? Do I have to go to bed now?" Before I had a chance to remind her that it was already past her bedtime, a little man with a bike helmet and a towel for a cape was squeezing through the doorway. He had escaped from his room. He climbed up on my lap, gave me a good night kiss, and asked "Mom? Can I be a superhero tomorrow?" "Okay, Joseph, but only if I can be a superhero too!" I answered, this time uninterrupted.

"Okay, mom, but only if you let me wear your boots!"

"Good night, Joseph," I said.

"Mom, can I tell you a Jesus story?"

Before Joseph could finish telling me about Jesus and His

amazing water-walking powers, Josh appeared in the room and scooped Joseph up for tickles and tuck-ins. He also grabbed his guitar and took it upstairs, too. I closed my eyes as his peaceful songs filled the air and lulled a house full of children to sleep.

PACKING AGAIN

We were up late again, this time packing for Josh's flight. In the rare silence of our home, we talked about the new dream. We dreamed of finding a house that was big enough to hold our family and big enough to be a mission house, too. We spoke again about moving to a place where we can live the dream that began when I was a teenager in Mexico, working among the orphans. And then I listened as my husband once again brought our lives before our Lord who never fails. Once again, we were laying down our lives and holding on to all the promises of God. Josh held my hands in his and entrusted our next mission into God's hands. With all this love surrounding me, my heart was at peace.

As Josh zipped up his backpack I realized that we would soon be packing up everything that couldn't be replaced and selling or giving away everything else. We weren't just leaving behind our furniture and dishes here in Italy but hopefully a few changed lives, too.

Everything was changing, actually. The sun was setting on our time in Italy, and I was beginning to feel a change coming over me, too. I looked at Josh, such a devoted and loving father, such a strong and faithful husband. We didn't even know what country we would call our home in the near future, and I was tempted to give in to fear. But in that moment, peace came over me as we stayed up talking late into the night.

Once again, we would trade all that we had for a new chapter in life that we knew nothing about. We both knew that God's plans for us were far better than anything we could ever dream up, and as we looked back over the years, we knew we could smile at the future. We would never lack anything of true value as long as we trusted in God with our whole hearts. Our lives had been full of unexpected moments and unbelievable stories that had brought us to this uncanny moment of confident uncertainty.

We talked about the times in the past when we had been in this same place. No, not in a house on a hill in a village in Italy. But in those moments in life where one season was passing and a new one was coming, and everything was happening all at once. Nothing seemed certain except that it was time to let go of the past and hold on tighter to God and to each other.

HOUSE HUNTING TIME AGAIN

A week later, Josh came home from Ukraine with stories to tell and a heart full of faith. We quickly bought plane tickets for everyone to go on the next trip, and suddenly it was house hunting time again. After just a little more than a year in Italy, we were leaving our home high on a hill, overlooking the city of Montebelluna. A new country, a new adventure, a new dream. We immediately started filling our bags and suitcases with the things we couldn't easily replace in our new home, this time packing even lighter than before. With nine children following behind, this was an almost impossible task. But we could bring only what we could carry with us onto an airplane. I quickly learned that packing this way was more about leaving things behind than about deciding what would fit inside these twenty-two pieces of luggage.

We were moving to Ukraine in just eight short days. The church bells rang as the last leaves of autumn were swept away and scattered by the late November wind. Everything in my life felt so scattered actually, so out of place. It was the first time I had packed up our family not knowing where our next home would be. It seemed like a crazy thing to do with a family of eleven . . . maybe twelve. I still hadn't taken the long walk into town to buy a pregnancy test. Honestly, I had a feeling that the stress of our lives was what was messing up my monthly cycle, not a new baby, though. My life felt upside down again, but I had been there before. This was the place where faith and vision met, and it was a good place to be.

Josh and Isaac left Italy earlier that day with 140 pounds of luggage and plane tickets to Romania. We had many belongings to give away and knew that the poor families and orphans in Romania would love to have many of the things we couldn't bring with us. As far as I knew, we were not moving to

Romania, but in my life, anything could happen. My husband was always full of big, new ideas, and so far they had all been good. I just never knew what he would think of next. When they left, the plan had been for Josh and Isaac to take the heavy load of winter coats and other warm things to the Romanian orphans they were visiting that weekend. They would be back home with us on Sunday—just a few days before we all left again to go to Ukraine. Together. That was the plan.

I took a break from packing to write. As I pulled out the laptop and began capturing some of the stories from the past two weeks, Anna perched herself on the back of the couch beside me to read. What book? My eyes fell on the page she was reading: Psalm 139. The text was about God's Spirit and how he is always with us wherever we go. I needed to remember that. Apparently my 14-year-old daughter did, too.

Estera, our 12 year old, was busy sticking Post-it notes on the bookshelf in long rows. A closer look revealed she was working on her multiplication facts, determined to master her nines and sevens.

"I should know all these by now, but I keep forgetting! Ugggh!" she said when she noticed me looking at her. Eleven-month-old Ember watched her and giggled while she grabbed at the little yellow papers.

My ten year old, Rachel, was playing math games with Joseph. It was the day after Thanksgiving—*why all the math and reading,* I wondered. I think they had learned if Mom sees them busy learning they won't be asked to do house work. They did love learning, but from the look of the living room, there was a lot of packing, sorting, and cleaning to do! But what could I do? Tell them to stop reading the Bible and stop memorizing math facts so they could fold these clothes? No, not me. I picked up a pen and paper to make my list of things to bring and then found myself writing again. The three middle girls were playing together in their room, their happy voices echoing down the hallway as Mozart's "Concerto 17" filled the air with peace. The packing could wait.

Like most Americans around the world, we were enjoying a day of leftovers. Pie for breakfast, turkey for lunch, and dinner wasn't planned yet. Unlike most Americans, our cranberry sauce was made from lemons and cherries, and our pumpkin pies were made from sweet potatoes, but no one could tell the difference. Cranberries and pumpkins weren't typical Italian foods.

I thought again about how impossible it all seemed that we would move our family of eleven across the ocean. I thought about that a lot lately as we prepared to move again. Where would we be now if we had not read that book a few years ago that helped us set up our online business? How could we have supported our family in these far-off places if we hadn't been able to work just a few hours a week publishing the series of 16 unusual workbooks designed to teach dyslexic children how to read? I thought about Josh, too, working 50 hours a week just last year, always late because he was trying to squeeze in every possible opportunity, and how we just dropped out of the rat race and moved to Northern Italy to begin a new life, a new mission.

Life had slowed down significantly in Italy. Josh and Isaac attended an international Bible college and both got involved with the music ministry in a local church. I spent most of my time learning how to manage a large family without a car, superstore, dryer, stove, and backyard. The kids enjoyed some awesome homeschool field trips to places like Venice, Austria, and the Dolomite Mountains. And we all learned how to live in harmony in a smaller house.

But we were ready to move on. We all wanted to help orphans, and that is why we were making plans to go house hunting in Ukraine, a nation with 30,000 children living in orphanages. When we arrived, we planned to stay with my parents in their two-bedroom apartment in L'Viv until we found our next home.

So, on the day after Thanksgiving in 2013, I was deciding what to pack for our next adventure, what to carry with us through that next open window. Once again we were simplifying. After bringing half a ton of luggage with us just a year before, for this move each of the children could bring only what they were willing to wear or carry. They each had a backpack and a small suitcase with wheels that could be stowed in the overhead compartment or under their seats as we traveled. All of my own clothing and personal things would have to fit in just one suitcase.

With nine children to pack for, I discovered that their needs trumped my wants.

Something Borrowed

I am wearing borrowed shoes
Shirt and jacket from the second-hand bag, too
And my jeans fit perfectly, I think
before I lost the baby fat last spring

I'm carrying a borrowed backpack
Filled with my greatest earthly treasures and a snack
My Bible, journals, and a book of stories tied with string
Stories that I wrote when I was just sixteen.

I have a pair of warm gloves and a wallet with no cash
I have an empty coffee cup and feeling that will pass
I have an empty book and pencil here with me
I hope there is just enough change to buy my coffee

I packed a suitcase this morning, and gave the rest away
I'll take less, just what I think I will need on the next adventure
I prefer simplicity to clutter, and the burden that stuff brings
I'd rather have children, than expensive earthly things.

I would rather fill my books with memories together,
I would rather fill my children's hearts with lasting treasures.
I would rather explore the world and hear the church bells ring,
Than have a stable home filled with precious things.

Photo albums, facebook posts, and borrowed boots.
Holding hands and walking in the rain.
Train tickets, plane tickets, bus tickets, too.
Packing light, dreaming big, still in my daughter's shoes.

THE THINGS WE LEAVE BEHIND

I was sitting in the small café at the top of the hill thinking through all our last minute plans. The TV was a little too loud and kept distracting me. It was time to make my final list. *What else did we need to pack?* Four guitars, a violin, a keyboard, some portable drums, Isaac's recording studio, four laptop computers, a printer, about 100 of the world's best books, my journals, my scrapbooks, some pottery to remember Italy by, sheets and blankets, my sewing machine, pots, pans, Isaac's chef knives, Josh's chess game, and my birthing pool and a bag of newborn supplies, just in case. And that was packing light. I could also see that I should wait to do the final packing the following week once the guys returned, since most of the big stuff belonged to them. The list of things we were leaving behind was much longer. The challenge and the fun would be selling what we could and giving the rest away, just as most of it had been given to us.

I had crossed the ocean eleven times and had lived in twenty-two houses. I had learned that all I really needed—besides food, love, and clothing—was my Bible, a notebook, and a comfortable pair of shoes that could handle any kind of weather. Sometimes, an umbrella came in handy, but who wanted to carry an umbrella wherever they went? When I walked out my door, I just expected the clouds to break, the sun to peek out, and the thunder to quiet. God knew for the past several months that I had no car and had to walk two miles just to get to a real grocery store. If it looked like rain, I had learned to wait for a sunny day and to be creative and content with the things that I had.

This wasn't necessarily a practical way to live, but I loved the freedom and fresh air. An inconvenient life had suited me well, actually. The best things in life were often inconvenient, and I had only two hands. With one hand, I held tightly to my husband, and with the other, I held a paintbrush, a pen, a ladle, or the chubby little hand of a toddler. The umbrellas of life were not always necessary—unless you were a teenager falling in love. But I've already shared that story.

Sometimes, life seemed more about what we left behind than what we brought along, so I wanted to master the art of letting go. The key, I learned, was figuring out what was worth holding on to and what I needed to leave behind, pass along, or give away. Learn the art of letting go, and life becomes simple, beautiful and meaningful. Just as long as we don't let go of the things that matter most, like our families, our faith, our purity, and our eternal callings.

As I finished writing my list and pondering my life, I glanced up at the TV. I saw a scene of thousands of people waving flags, Ukrainian flags. They were angry. I tried hard to decipher the Italian spoken by the news reporter. I watched as they showed scenes from cities all over Ukraine, including L'viv. There was a revolution beginning, and a million people had already taken to the streets and city squares to protest. The people were rising up in opposition to the government, and many people feared that peaceful revolution could lead to a brutal war.

How could we trade the peace of Italy for a country on the brink of war? There I was sipping coffee, like everything was normal. I pushed thoughts of war and revolution out of my mind. We had already bought the tickets, after all. For that moment I felt courageous and frightened all at once.

Italian Cafe

Another Tuesday in a cafe, on a hill in Italy
My home is just a step away, on a hill in Italy
I have a latte coming my way as I write my silent thoughts and fears
The sunlight breaks now through the shade to find me here.

Add the sugar, stir the silver spoon
Now the music begins to softly play
Hallelujah, Hallelujah is the tune
The words bring peace to my troubled day.

When I leave here, it's time to pack and go
A new city, country, and a new-found home
To an unsettled land that lies beneath the snow
So many things in life are still unknown.

I see the news, protests, and revolutions.
And many dread the thought of civil war
Protect us God, and grant us Your protection
We look to You, it's You that we live for.

Here I am, I feel at peace, my coffee's gone
On a hill in Italy, where nothing now seems wrong
But soon we'll cross the mountains, and leave the quiet shore
To where a million rise in unrest fearing war.

THE CHANGING VIEW

We stood together by the window, Josh's arms around me. A chill was in the air. The last leaves of autumn twirled on the frigid wind, and the sun sank into the west as the moon rose in the east. Moonlight glowed over November's final pink roses, and suddenly the western clouds turned from grey to red to purple, vanishing behind the far-off mountains. We stopped to catch our breath at the beauty of the silver light falling on the distant crowns of snow. Everything looked a little different than it had just a week ago, and nothing was like it would be in just a few days more. It was the brief moment where two seasons were merging and passing.

As we watched the leaves fall from the maple trees outside our window—the rich reds, the yellows, the brilliant bursts of orange—we didn't worry that we would never see green again. Why? Because we had witnessed spring before, and we knew without a doubt it would come again and bring more green leaves with it. We were not hopeless, nor did we mourn the passing of the last pink rose. We knew that a new year would bring new life and dozens of pretty pink buds would grace the rose bush once again. As we looked out to the vineyards on the village edge, we saw the bare branches of the vines, but we knew they were simply resting. They would bear fruit again. We were certain.

While we packed up our family to move to Ukraine, we began to see more and more images of revolution posted on Facebook by friends living in L'viv. The city had been peaceful earlier in the fall when we heard God's call and decided to move. The needs of the orphans had pulled on the cords of our hearts, calling us to come and leave Italy behind. But now we weren't sure what was waiting for us in our new home.

I felt so safe and at peace as Josh held me close and stroked my hair, planting sweet little kisses on my cheek, my nose, my ears. I could feel his joy, his anticipation, his fearlessness, his sense of wonder as he propped his feet on our packed suitcase. His confidence had a way of calming my fears. Just one more day and we would be on a plane to Ukraine. Josh would help me get settled in Ukraine with my parents for a few days, then he would return to Italy to finish packing and cleaning with the older girls. Hopefully by the time the rest of the family arrived in Ukraine, we would have a home to move into.

I would be house hunting without Josh this time.

Alone in Ukraine

Dear Joshua,

I'm looking out the window of our new apartment over the beautiful City of L'viv. I am here on the fourth floor, and I can see the city disappearing into the night from my perspective. Christmas lights twinkle in every window, and snowflakes flutter through the air.

As the snow falls I remember another chilly December day exactly 17 years ago! It was the day you asked me to be your bride, and I said yes!

Life together has been so sweet, so full of joy, and such an adventure. I really do love you more and more with each passing year. I love being yours and raising a family with you. When I think about all that we share, and all that we have been through, and how passionate you are about living what we believe . . . I just know that we are living life the way life was meant to be lived.

I look around and see so many broken families, so many struggling marriages, so many broken hearted people who once had so much hope, and I look at us, and wonder how it is we are so blessed. I'm so thankful that you read the Bible to me and pray with me nearly every night. I know that we are both far from perfect, but at least we know how to forgive.

I am so thankful to be yours in this life. I am thankful for your faith, I am thankful for the way you lead our family, I am thankful for your soft heart and contagious smile. I am thankful for the way you treat me like a princess (a very good thing that you learned from your dad) and how you always have time to spend with each child, lavishing each one in love and always leading them to Jesus.

Today I am missing you. You are still in Italy, packing, and I'm here in Ukraine.

Here I am, looking out over a cobblestone street, looking out over the rooftops. Here we are, ready to begin again. A new city, a new country, a new mission, a new language. Counting down the days, the hours, the minutes . . . to be with you.

I Love You,

Sarah

I Love You. Sarah...

AFTERWORD

When we arrived, the city of L'viv spoke life and depth and mystery to us. My heart could hear the city yearning for hope, redemption, and healing at the same time. The cobblestone streets beneath my feet whispered to me that these streets would lead my family to our next home. My mom and dad were waiting for us there. And so were the orphans. But the fighting and the violence were growing worse. Within just a few weeks, thousands of angry protesters gathered on the streets, building fires, waving flags, and demanding change.

I was afraid, but the fear was overshadowed by something greater, so we went. But we kept 11 backpacks lined up by the door, just in case war broke out and we would have to flee quickly. And we prayed for the peace of Ukraine.

We quickly got involved in a ministry to orphans, and our whole family enjoyed sharing music, art projects, Bible stories, and birthday parties with the children. Working with orphans was truly a calling we loved! The revolution grew worse in western Ukraine, but L'viv became more peaceful, so we planned to stay long term.

Just a few short months after we arrived in Ukraine, our visas were set to expire. Josh and I took Isaac, Anna, and Ember to Hungary to apply for new visas for the whole family. The other six children stayed with my parents. We expected to be back within a couple of weeks. While we were gone, however, the rioting drew very close to our home. My parents could even see burning buildings from their apartment window. We decided we needed to bring the rest of the children to Hungary with us while we waited for the visas, so Josh went back to get them. We didn't realize that once we were all back together again outside of Ukraine that it would be several months before we would return. When we left Hungary, we spent time in Bosnia, Croatia, England, Germany, Austria, and Portugal.

Right now, we have round trip tickets to Florida for the holidays and then back to Europe in the Spring. Baby number ten will be arriving shortly after Christmas while we are visiting Josh's family in Florida. Ember will have the joy of being a big sister, too, and everyone is talking about baby names.

We don't know where we will make our next home when we cross the ocean in the spring. But for now, we are enjoying the view from the windows wherever we find ourselves.

We are together, and we are loved.

MY INSPIRATION

My mother passed me a paintbrush, a love for children, and a cookbook. My grandpa Eugene was an artist too, but not only an artist who passed me a paintbrush; he was a master gardener, who passed me a shovel. My father was a pastor who passed a Bible to me, and he also passed me a baseball, a camera, a guitar, and a fishing pole. My Aunt Susie passed me a chicken, a live chicken from her flock, and she let me collect eggs, too. She also passed me a saddle after I climbed her fence and rode her pony bareback in the muddy pasture.

My beautiful grandma Nana passed me her beauty secrets, and my Aunt Michelle passed me her needle and thread, her car keys, and her glue-gun. My grandma Marian passed along a love for all things beautiful and sweet. My sister Sunny passed along her love for little children. My sister Linda passed me her lipstick, her tootsie roll, and a "get out of jail free" card when I was in a really tight spot during a Monopoly game. She also invited me to be with her during the birth of her second child and passed me her courage and taught me how to handle pain without fear.

My sister Charity passed me a newborn kitten, a thin mint cookie, and my first blank book. My little sister Heather passed along with her friendship and was there for me through the hardest moments of growing up, saying goodbye, moving to new places, and starting over. She was always nearby when I needed someone to pass me a rock, a stick, or a shovel when we were building bridges over streams or squirrel houses in the woods.

My friend Amy passed me the dice, the cards, and the baby bunnies. My 5th grade teacher, Mrs. Sally Abney, passed along the assurance that I could be an artist, a writer, or even an astronaut. My Sunday school teacher, Mike Bucher, and his wife, Sheila, passed me a new born baby and their love for children. During my teen years, my friend Julie passed me the microphone. My youth pastor, John Hwang, passed many songs along to me, and he also passed along a love for reading my Bible. Pastor Chuck Smith passed me a plane ticket to Hungary so I could help a missionary family with their children.

Laura Anderson passed me a dream of raising a family on the mission field, and Christine Dente passed me my first organic salad and my first Starbucks Coffee. Nancy Campbell passed along the courage to open my heart and share my story with others. The Markey family passed me a vision to expect great things from God, to follow Him to the ends of the earth, and trust the Lord with our children, no matter how many. Some of my most precious friends, Diahann, Leslie, Lynn, Melanie, Allison, Amber, Candace, Barb, Carol, Hope, Nancy, Rose, Debbie, and Autumn, showed up unexpectedly in my life, just in time to share countless blessings with me over the years as we passed prayers, funny stories, babies, and ideas back and forth. We learned together about how to become women of faith. We helped each other to be better wives, patient mothers, compassionate friends, and inspiring teachers, and then we said goodbye.

WHERE IS THE BROWN FAMILY TODAY?
Stop by www.StillSmiling.net to find out!

READ MORE BY SARAH BROWN:
Visit www.ThinkingTreePress.com for more books
by Sarah Janisse Brown and a list of her wonderful
educational resources for children with Dyslexia, Asperger's,
ADHD, and other Learning Challenges.

NEW IN 2015:
Sarah's Scrapbook, Sarah's Sketchbook,
and a new magazine for girls created by Sarah
and her teen daughters Anna & Estera!

Made in the USA
Columbia, SC
10 May 2020